IMAGES
of America

LINCOLN CITY
AND THE
TWENTY MIRACLE MILES

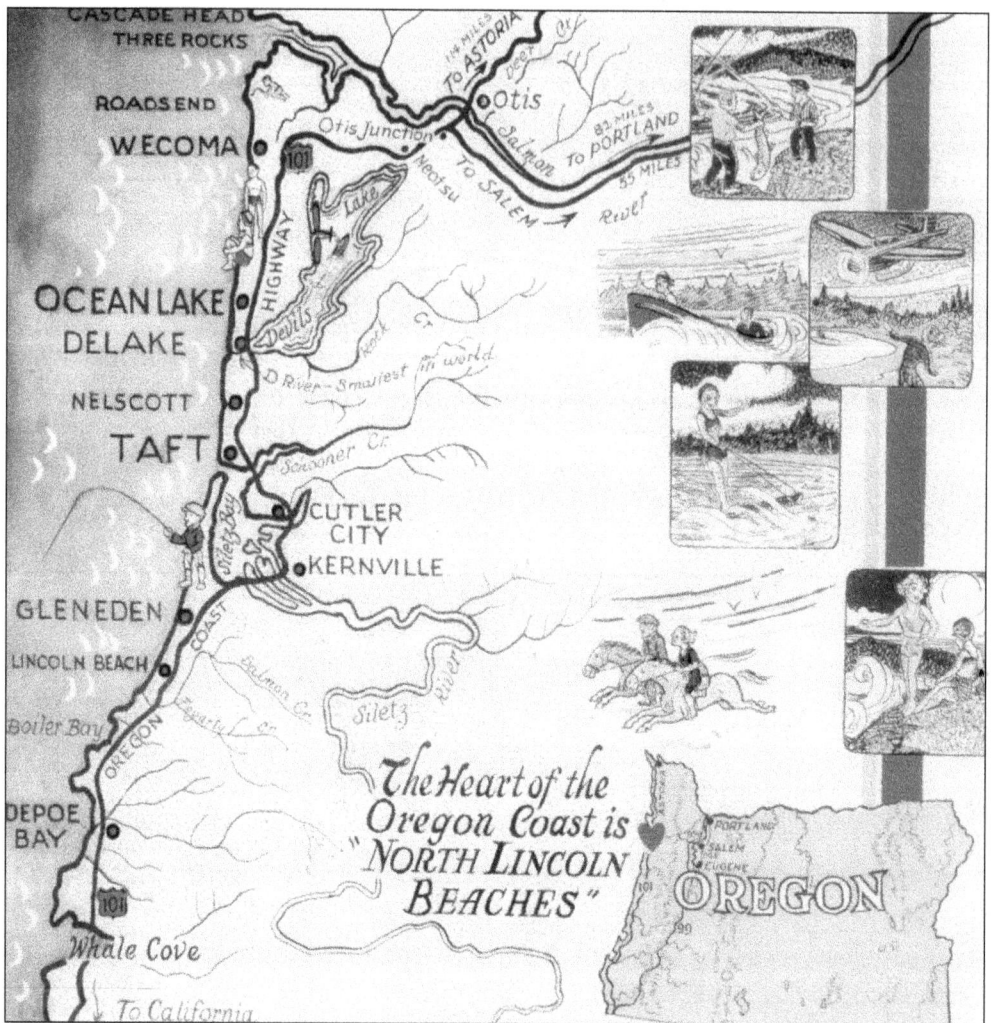

This illustrated map, designed to bring tourists to north Lincoln County, shows the location of the towns included in the Twenty Miracle Miles. From Cascade Head to Depoe Bay, they hugged the shore, with the exception of Otis and Rose Lodge in the northeast. Illustrations include the many activities that could be enjoyed by visitors to this part of the Oregon coast. (Courtesy of the North Lincoln County Historical Museum.)

ON THE COVER: This c. 1927 photograph shows the service station at the Nelscott Auto Park, one of the first in north Lincoln County, with an unidentified attendant standing in front of the pumps. The station and auto park were owned and operated by Anna and George Cushing. Many auto parks and service stations started up in the late 1920s in response to the high demand created by coastal visitors. (Courtesy of the North Lincoln County Historical Museum.)

IMAGES
of America

LINCOLN CITY
AND THE
TWENTY MIRACLE MILES

Anne Jobbe Hall

ARCADIA
PUBLISHING

Published by Arcadia Publishing
Charleston, South Carolina

Library of Congress Catalog Card Number: 2008921574

For all general information contact Arcadia Publishing at:
Telephone 843-853-2070
Fax 843-853-0044
E-mail sales@arcadiapublishing.com
For customer service and orders:
Toll-Free 1-888-313-2665

Visit us on the Internet at www.arcadiapublishing.com

Dedicated to Mildred Harmon Salazar,
who preserved the memories of so many.
Mildred, we will always remember you.

CONTENTS

ACKNOWLEDGMENTS

My respect and gratitude go to the people whose images fill these pages. Although their everyday lives are seldom preserved in history books, they are the people who lived on the land, gave birth to their children here, hunted, fished, made homes, planted gardens, and helped each other survive in a harsh environment.

The people who donated these images to the North Lincoln County Historical Museum are to be commended and thanked as well. Their thoughtfulness and effort have made it possible for these photographs to be woven into the larger fabric of this region's history.

I am also deeply grateful to all the people, generous with their time and talent, whose work insured the history of this area would be preserved and remembered. The North Lincoln Pioneer Association, led by Earl Nelson, defined the mission to capture local history by publishing the first volume of the *Pioneer History of North Lincoln County*.

Mildred Harmon Salazar, an intrepid teacher, librarian, and historian, continued the work by conducting oral history interviews of early settlers during a 30-year period. That effort would have been more than enough, but she carried forth the work by transcribing, editing, indexing, and publishing her interviews. Thanks to Mildred, her good friend and right hand, Merilynn Merritt Webb, and the Pioneer Association, we have the second and third volumes of the *Pioneer History of North Lincoln County*.

The North Lincoln County Historical Museum (NLCH) continues to build on this solid foundation by maintaining an archives and research library, and by exhibiting artifacts. Without this organization, this book and future histories would flounder. My warmest thanks go to the board of directors of the museum, led by Pres. Jean Majoska. Their commitment and hard work have made the museum what it is today.

NLCH Museum volunteers can never be thanked enough for doing those time-consuming tasks that keep the museum functioning. Special thanks to Danell Martin, who edited this book and gave timely encouragement. Finally, many thanks go to Ann Murdock, my assistant, who makes work easier no matter what the task.

INTRODUCTION

The natural beauty of the central Oregon coast rivals any place in the world, but life has never been easy along this stretch of Pacific shore. Residents contest with winds that pull up trees and tear down buildings. The same rain that blesses the land with abundant green life at times blows sideways in sheets until every river, creek, and stream floods its banks. Imagine coming to such an environment with everything you owned, wagon and horses sunk deep in the mud. Imagine once you got there, clearing the land in the rain, milking cows in the rain, fishing and living for months in the rain. You had to want it very much. You had to think the beauty and freedom of the place was worth the effort it took to live there.

The story of this land, shaped by man and nature, is compelling in its drama and heartwarming in its humor and human experience. Although the photographs in this book were never meant to capture the whole story, collected together they paint a picture of a shared time and experience, of the history and heritage that gives us a sense of place.

Unfortunately, we have no photographs of the first people to inhabit the land, no pictures or other documents to tell us about their lives. Shell middens and accounts of white explorers tell only a small part of their history. A peaceful people, they hunted elk and deer in the forested hills, fished in the many waters, and gathered food from the land and sea. Long houses with large central fireplaces sheltered them during the winter, while capes of water-repellent grass allowed them to work and hunt outside. At the beginning of the 1800s, exploration of the Pacific Northwest by Europeans looking for a northwest passage brought devastating disease to the area. By the late 1840s, only a small remnant of the original people remained. Basket making, dancing, story telling, gaming, and living as a friend of nature are the cultural heritage of these people.

The first photographs of Native Americans presented here are of the people taken from their homes in northern California and southern Oregon, the people who became the Confederated Tribes of the Siletz Indians. These people, from diverse tribes, were brought to the distant, inhospitable Coast Reservation. After a bitter journey and transition in which thousands died, the tribes began to successfully clear and farm the land. They built homes and schools while learning to adopt a way of life compatible with government policy. But soon they were asked to once again change their way of life and adopt another foreign concept, land ownership. A presidential order decreed that each tribal member take a tiny bit of reservation land as his "allotment," with the remainder of reservation lands returned to government hands. At first the Confederated Tribes resisted, but after realizing they had no real choice, the people took what was offered.

Some allotments were sold and some lost to taxes, while a few tribal members claimed and lived on their land. It is amazing that these allotment holders got along so well with the homesteaders that came shortly after, in the late 1890s, but they did, becoming kind and helpful neighbors.

Unlike the native people, homesteaders were ready and eager to take up individual parcels of land, make improvements, and become landowners. To the homesteaders, land ownership meant independence and freedom from poverty. It meant the freedom to create a life as good as a person's heart and hands could make it. These people came with enthusiasm and determination. Though their lives were hard, they shared many good things and lived together in harmony. A glimpse of their lives can be seen in these photographs.

Once paved roads were built, people came to the area who were interested in developing and living in coastal towns. Ingenious and adaptive, they used natural resources to pioneer fishing, dairy, and logging industries. They worked hard—building homes, schools, businesses, and, eventually, bridges and highways—but their spirit of fun is what is so evident in these photographs. The towns they built would grow to reflect the character of the residents, each town uniquely beautiful yet so interconnected they have been described as "a string of pearls."

Completion of coastal roads meant that visitors began arriving at this formerly isolated shore. People came to the beach to enjoy themselves while escaping valley heat. Sometimes they came for just one day, but more often they stayed and camped, taking advantage of whatever food and guest services were available. Before long, those services became the area's economic mainstay. Soon business and community leaders tried to think of ways to attract visitors to this area of the coast rather than another. Tourism promotions like the Redhead Round-Up and the Devils Lake Regatta attracted visitors by offering something special, something not found elsewhere. Photographs of these promotions and the people who created them provide a fascinating look at American life during the first part of the 20th century.

Eventually, town leaders saw the wisdom of combining resources to create a combined city with shared police, fire, and water services. In the mid-1950s, townspeople worked together successfully to create a statewide tourism campaign, defining the area as the Twenty Miracle Miles. Yet when it came to combining the towns, it was difficult to convince people to give up some of their individuality for the benefits a larger city could provide.

After a process of discussion and assessment, along with several failed attempts, Cutler City, Taft, Nelscott, Delake, and Oceanlake incorporated as one city on March 3, 1965. When it came to naming the town, the spirit of cooperation grew thin. No one wanted the new city to reflect a bias toward any one of the combined towns, so a contest was held to find a new name. "Lincoln City," submitted by schoolchildren, was chosen from among the entries. Photographs included here show how Lincoln City was born and how it continues to evolve as a beach community. Today's residents, diverse in age and background, still care about one another and still endeavor to make this area the Twenty Miracle Miles.

One

NATIVE PEOPLES

Native Americans inhabited this area of the central Oregon coast for thousands of years prior to white settlement. Although little archeological evidence remains today, it is known that these relatively peaceful peoples shared a mild climate and plentiful foods obtained through hunting deer and elk, fishing for salmon and eel, and harvesting nut and berry crops. Groups are characterized as bands rather than tribes, since their organization had more to do with family relationships than governing. The native people of the Salmon River basin were a Salish-speaking subbranch of the northern Tillamook Indians, while the people of the Siletz River were more related to the Yaquina Indians to the south. This photograph of Chief John Williams, a Siletz Indian, shows him in full regalia around 1930.

Shell middens, Native American refuse piles, marked the sites of native villages and encampments. When examined today, they provide considerable evidence about the daily lives of native people. Most shell middens found along the coast were located at the mouths of rivers, where fish and seafood were most plentiful. An enormous shell midden, found in the late 1800s in Taft, indicated hundreds of years of native habitation along Siletz Bay. Unfortunately, that shell midden disappeared when 20th-century pioneers used the composite material to pave roads. The two women pictured here are members of the Confederated Tribes of Siletz Indians, in traditional dress. The unidentified woman on the left is wearing a basket hat. Basket hat designs were unique to the maker. They identified the wearer by tribe based on the type of weave, the colors and materials used, and the overall pattern or design. Secret symbols woven into the basket also identified the wearer. The woman on the left is Tootsie Smith-Simmons, whose relatives are still active in tribal government today.

In 1849, Lt. Theodore Talbot reported a much diminished Native American population along Siletz Bay. When his party attempted to cross the Siletz River, a Native American man who aided them told them he and one other man, along with their families, were the only native people left in the bay area. This photograph shows Siletz Indian twins John and Jack Logan in their cradle baskets. (Courtesy of the Oregon Historical Society.)

On November 9, 1855. Pres. Franklin Pierce signed an executive order establishing the Coast Reservation along the Central Oregon Coast. The order set in motion the relocation of Native Americans residing in Southern Oregon and Northern California, forever changing the lives of these native peoples. Shown here is "Indian John," a Siletz Indian thought to be 116 years old at the time of this photograph.

The first relocated Native Americans arrived in 1856 at the mouth of the Salmon River. Poverty and disease diminished their population rapidly because of the infrequent and insufficient supplies and foodstuffs promised by the government. Louisa Logan, seen here at an Indian Ceremony in 1924, is from a well-known family of Siletz Indians who had an allotment at Roads End. Logan Road is named for this family.

Despite hardships, by the spring of 1857 more than 300 acres were in cultivation on reservation lands. Log cabins, an office, storehouse, warehouse, drugstore, "issue house," cookhouse, blacksmith shop, school, and hospital were all under construction at that time. Seen here from left to right are Siletz Indian allotment holders Gladys Cason Cutler, John and Jane Baxter, Charles G. Davis, and Mary and George Cutler holding an impressive fish catch.

In 1887, the government passed the Dawes Act, giving the president the authority to impose land ownership on Native Americans, an idea at odds with Indian culture and philosophy. Allotments consisted of individual land parcels held in trust by the government for 25 years. Jakie and Sissie Johnson's allotment covered most of the Taft bay front. This photograph shows an unidentified man, left, with Sissie in the middle and Jakie on the right.

Basket making was an essential skill in most Native American cultures. Both form and function were important in the design of each basket. Siletz Indian Minnie Lane is seen here standing among a variety of her handcrafted baskets. Note the double-handled baskets at the front. The double handle is a distinctive characteristic of baskets made by the Confederated Tribes of the Siletz Indians. (Courtesy of the Oregon Historical Society.)

The Siletz Indians did not accept the Dawes Act, also known as the General Allotment Act, until 1894. Each tribal member was given 80 acres of former reservation land, half of what a homesteader could claim after improving the land and three year's residence. In total, the allotted land amounted to 44,459 acres, a small portion of the original reservation lands. In the early days of settlement, Native American allotment holders and early settlers got on well together, with few exceptions. Often native people, who had themselves learned how to survive on this rain-soaked coast, helped the settlers. They taught them fishing, hunting and gathering techniques, how to cross Siletz Bay on horseback, and other skills needed in this environment. For a number of years, settlers and tribal members celebrated the Fourth of July together with annual picnics. This photograph shows settlers and Siletz Indians enjoying one of these picnics c. 1924.

Two

BUILDING A LIFE

Settlement came late to the central Oregon coast. Consequently, many early pioneers and homesteaders lived well into the 20th century. A gathering of all those who homesteaded or came to this area before 1925 is the occasion for this Taft meeting of the North Lincoln County Pioneers on May 6, 1956. Seated are, from left to right, (first row) Charles F. Robertson, Mary Robertson, John Affolter, Mary Plummer, Anna Murray, Charles Davis, Gladys Davis, Sarah Muir, Gertrude Crawford, Gertrude Tibbets, Mata Slater, and Helen Neimi; (second row) Mrs. Dave McNeal, Mary Horner, Esther Hill, Myrtle Hallock, Mrs. Gus Ketola, Mrs. August Johnson, Elsie Paul, Alvah Strome, Roy Horner, Georgia Bones, Ernest Bones, Ruby Parmele, Edgar Parmele, Lucy Turnbull, Robert Turnbull, and Netty Petterson; (third row) Frank Hallock, Walter McClintock, Dave McNeal, Lila Hallock, Mrs. Jim Sutton, Hattie Gnoss, Jim Sutton, Harvey Hill, Jack Fogarty, Wesley Bones, Rachel Strome, Gus Ketola, Art Beaver, and Lee Affolter.

Many Finns came to homestead the Oregon coast. Steamship companies advertised free land for those willing and able to work hard and endure a harsh environment. To someone born in Finland, this opportunity seemed like a dream. The land was like their native Finland with its rivers, lakes, trees, and familiar way of life. This photograph of the Victor Hill homestead on Devils Lake shows two families of Finnish homesteaders c. 1904.

Homesteaders had to establish a residence on a parcel of land to claim it as their own. The first problem they faced was how to get there. There were no ships or railroads to take them to the homesteads, often chosen from a plat map. This 1908 photograph shows (from left to right) Nettie Long, a Mrs. Miller, and Clyde Long with the kind of wagon used by homesteaders to bring all their household goods to the homestead.

16

Arriving in Portland by steamboat with all their belongings, homesteaders had to find a way to haul what they would need to a distant home in an untamed wilderness. Many hired or bought a horse and wagon for the trip, little knowing what a rough road they would have to travel to reach home. From left to right, Mr. and Mrs. C. O. Butterfield are seen here on horseback with George Parmele in 1904.

The trip from Salem took from five to six days with one stop in Willamina for the night and another in Pitner. The mud was so deep that the men had to put two mule teams on one wagon to take it to the top of a hill. This 1920 photograph shows wagons ready to haul hay to Delake with wheels sunk into the mud and beach sand.

When at last settlers caught their first sight of the blue Pacific Ocean, they rejoiced, knowing they were almost home. Driving their teams through the white sand, they found it as smooth as a paved highway after the "corduroy" road of timber and mud they had just traversed. In this c. 1916 photograph, an oxcart is being used by a Mrs. French to pick up supplies at the store in Taft.

Determination and the ability to keep going in the face of adversity were necessary characteristics of early pioneers. Once a pioneer reached his homestead, the real work began. After setting up tents needed until a home could be built, it took several weeks to clear a piece of land. A Mrs. McClintock is seen here preparing a meal in her tent home with her young daughter watching, far left.

Mr. and Mrs. Joe Mitchell, left, were Native American allotment holders who helped homesteaders adjust to a difficult way of life. Mr. Mitchell, known as "Corner" because he always sat in a corner, had a blacksmith shop. Mrs. Mitchell was a midwife. Both were well loved by the community. Their neighbors, Mr. and Mrs. Hellenbrand, are seen here standing in a doorway with their son Oscar, at far right.

Because travel was so difficult, road building became the number one priority for early pioneers. The effort to clear and level roads was worthwhile if it meant everyday life would be easier. This 1910 crew is building the road over Newton Hill in Neotsu. Pictured here are, from left to right, Harley Taylor, Joe Dowd, Harry Chatterton, Abe Logan, and Joshley Brown with Phil Etting directing the work, far right. The young boy is unidentified.

During the early pioneering days, waterways were easier courses for travel than roads. Those who lived along rivers especially preferred traveling by water. All people needed were a boat and a strong pair of arms to take them down the Siletz River to Taft, where they could stock up on food and supplies. George Parmele is seen at the oars in this 1904 photograph, taking relatives to town.

Homesteading required hard work, courage, faith in your fellow man, and a sense of humor. A good team of horses or mules was also a great help. Seen here plowing a field with his team of horses is Alvah Strome. Alvah and Rachel Strome, who homesteaded up the Siletz River, were known for always helping neighbors in need.

Before a homestead belonged to a pioneer, he had to meet federal regulations. The pioneer had to live on the property for three years, build a home, plant an orchard, and give evidence that he planned to make a life there. This 1903 photograph of the C. F. Robertson homestead on Schooner Creek shows a slash-and-burn fire used to clear the land for cultivation.

The pioneer home did not have many physical comforts for guests, but what it lacked in that respect it made up for in hospitality. Travelers knew they were always welcome to spend the night and that the latchstring was truly out for everyone. Although doors were never locked, nothing was stolen. This 1902 photograph shows visitors at the Dave Long homestead dressed in their best bib and tucker.

The land was fertile, and gardens provided plenty of vegetables, which, when cooked with venison, made wonderful meals. However, to make a garden, trees first had to be cut and the stumps removed before the soil was broken and crops planted. Heartbroken gardeners often found plants rotting from too much rain. Farmers had to learn to work with the seasons, and many homesteaders learned the hard way. Sometimes deer would eat the garden when it was about ready to be harvested, completely clearing out a garden overnight. Deer would also stand on their hind legs to get at the fruit in orchards. Connie and Myrtle Parmele, in the photograph at left, seem to have figured out how to garden successfully. The C. F. Robertson family is seen in the photograph below sitting on their porch in front of a lovely garden.

Pioneer children had to work hard on the homestead, as well as attend school. Yet most described their lives as idyllic during those years, when they could hunt, fish, and play in an environment as beautiful and wild as they were. Archie Stevens's children are seen here at the Havlin homestead playing with bows and arrows.

Children attended school in one-room schoolhouses. At first, schools were located in homes, with classes taught by a family member. All the children within a four-mile radius were considered eligible to attend, since it was thought reasonable that they walk that distance to and from school. From left to right are Bill Knight, Ray Seid, Charlie Immonen, Leonard Hespack, and Wayno Immonen outside of their school on Drift Creek.

23

George Parmele started the Johnson Intermediate School on his homestead property. He built the schoolhouse and hired Charles Butterfield to teach. This interior view of the school on Drift Creek shows Butterfield standing amidst his students: Olive and Ethel Parmele, far left corner, Myrtle, Edgar, Carrie, and Hoyt Parmele with Clarence Lockwood at the first table, and the Polander children at the table on the far right.

Homes were patterned after the log buildings of Finland. Logs were surfaced or adzed on two sides with the ends cut to interlock. The wood was natural, never painted. In later years, people built cedar shake homes. Sometimes they covered logs with split boards placed horizontally like clapboards, and other times they covered them with shakes. This photograph of the Arthur Beaver homestead shows his cabin covered in hand-hewn shakes.

Hunting for meat was a necessary part of pioneer subsistence. Deer and elk were plentiful in this area, but smaller game like rabbit, raccoon, and even squirrel provided a welcome change from salmon. About to set out, this hunting party appears to be enjoying the task ahead as they stand in front of the Toberer cabin on Drift Creek in 1910.

As roads improved, more and more automobiles appeared, replacing the horse and wagon. However, services like gasoline and tires were still largely unavailable until the late 1920s. This 1910 photograph shows Mike Schroeder, left, and an unidentified friend with their car, missing a wheel and broken down on the roadside plucking chickens. The handwritten caption on this photograph reads, "Stuck but not without resources."

Pioneers dressed up whenever they made a trip to town, even when picking up supplies or going to the beach for fun. This party of unidentified picnickers is especially dressed up for an Easter Sunday outing in 1902, complete with hats and gloves. The location for the picnic is the point where the Salmon River empties into the ocean just below Cascade Head.

Even in the 1920s, this well-dressed group enjoys an outing at the beach. Earl Nelson, son of Nelscott founder Charles Nelson, took this c. 1927 photograph of friends and relatives. In the front row, George Cushing is about to get clobbered by Lloyd Burdick and Nannie Nelson. In the back row are, from left to right, Anna Cushing, Nannie Nelson, Mary Burdick, and Ernie Burdick.

Until the 1930s, most people lived outside of town. Women complained that they were isolated from one another, spending months at a time with only their husbands and children for company and conversation. When the Community Kitchen was built in 1927, women's clubs began to meet there regularly to plan local programs and events. This group of unidentified women is seen outside the Community Kitchen rehearsing for a community play.

When groups of single men or women lived or stayed together for a period of time it was known locally as "batching." Seen here outside of a "batching" cabin after an all-night dance in Taft are, from left to right, Laila Hill Hallock, Sylvia Liswig, Sylvia Johnson, Laura Hill, Lydia Hill, Julie Liswig, and teacher Adeline "Alli" Liswig.

This 1920 photograph shows, from left to right, fishing buddies Jasper Lewis, Ben Hur Lampman, Herman Jordan, and Don Avery. Ben Hur Lampman wrote, "When I think of the Siletz . . . I think of Jap Luse and the Sijota boys, gray fishermen . . . and I wish that I might live it again, and fish the mouth of Bear Creak at the first fall freshet, or Cedar Creek when the winter steelhead are there."

Until the 1920s, this area was a fisherman's paradise. Salmon, so many one could scoop them up with a pitchfork, swam upriver to spawn. Trout, also plentiful, would be seen jumping out of the water to catch a fly skimming above the surface of the river. Alvah Strome is seen here, at far left with an unidentified man and child, pleased with his impressive fish catch.

At the mouth of the D River, the fish would "pour in" at times. A gaff hook mounted on a short pole and a lantern to see the fish fins sticking out of the water provided boys with all of the equipment they needed to catch from 50 to 100 fish a night. Seen here with a tremendous catch of catfish are Roy Snook, Walt Zellar, and Tony ?.

A wagon came by the Salmon River each morning to pick up salmon for the cannery. If the boys got a good catch, they waited all night for the wagon to pick up their fish and to collect their pay. The cannery paid 15¢ apiece for silversides and 30¢ to 35¢ each for Chinook salmon. George, left, and Orville Kangas caught these huge salmon on the Siletz River.

Along with fishing, the dairy industry provided homesteaders with a regular income. Most families had a cow or two, so milk, cream, and butter were plentiful. Women learned to make cheese and sell it. The lowlands of Taft and along the Siletz River were said to be the best dairy lands, but Pearl and Alex Fraser, seen here with their cows, did well in Otis near the Salmon River.

Especially in the early years, dairy farming showed great promise. In those days, most of the money was made shipping cream. The homesteader or farmer separated the whole milk, shipped the cream, and fed the skim milk to the pigs. Before the Frasers finished their dairy barn, seen here, Pearl milked the cows by hand, a labor-intensive job in any weather but much harder in the rain.

The dairy industry flourished in north Lincoln County until the late 1920s. In 1919, Matt Kangas and his family started a successful dairy business. The dairy was named the Spruce-Sylvan Dairy, but so many people referred to it as the Kangas Brothers Dairy they eventually changed the name. The Kangas Brothers Dairy had its own herd of high-test milk cows. Cows that were poor producers were eliminated from the herd. All the cows were double tested to insure their customers of the finest milk products available. Their refrigerated milk and cream garnered an outstanding reputation in the community for its high quality. In 1926, they established a delivery route. In the photograph above is one of the dairy's classy delivery trucks. At right, Christine (left) and Kathleen Kangas are pictured sitting on milk cans in front of the dairy.

Logging was dangerous work, involving long days of hard labor. It required knowledge, strength, and ingenuity, but it paid well. In fact, logging became the backbone of the Pacific Northwest economy. In the early days, men saved their money and bought timber to log. These independent loggers were known as "gyppos." Pictured standing on springboards with their double-handed cross saw and axes are George Kangas (left) and R. W. Hill.

The area was heavily timbered, and each man had to cut trees to clear land for farming or to build a house. Boys helped their fathers, learning how to fell trees from an early age. By the time they were old enough to get a job, they had learned a logger's many skills. The incredible size of trees felled with a cross saw is seen in this photograph below, c. 1898.

After the earliest era of logging with oxen and mule, steam-powered "donkey" engines were used to pull logs out of the woods. Skid roads were developed with logs laid vertically on the hills for the harvested logs to roll down. One man's job was to "grease the skids" to make them slick enough to speed logs downhill. This steam donkey and unidentified logging crew illustrate the difficulty of this process.

Log trucks only hauled one log at a time when trees were the size seen in this photograph. A log hauling parade was not an uncommon sight on Coast Highway through the 1950s. Loggers bragged about how they felled the biggest tree, topped the tallest spar, or pulled the biggest spruce ever with a "donkey." No trees could rival the giant Sitka spruce of Lincoln County.

During the 1930s, the Lincoln County Logging Company logged up the Siletz River. To transport the logs, tugboats hauled huge log rafts down the river to the ocean. From there, they went to mills either north to the Columbia River or south to Toledo. One of the most well known of these oceangoing tugs was the *Dodeca*, seen here being piloted over the Siletz bar by Capt. Martin Guchee.

The most dangerous part of a tug's journey out to sea was crossing the bar at the mouth of Siletz Bay, where ocean waves crashed over a sand spit. A captain had to wait for just the right tide level to cross, and sometimes he did not make it. Some tugboats were grounded on the bar and had to be rescued by other tugboats, as seen in this photograph.

Three

A String of Pearls

Few people today remember the town of Kernville, once a thriving community of fishermen, boatmen, and river dwellers. In the late 1800s, the Siletz River teemed with fish of all kinds, especially Silverback and Coho salmon. Daniel Kern thought this an ideal place to build a cannery. In 1896, he opened the Kern Brothers Packing Company on the north bank of the Siletz River, about 500 feet above Coyote Rock. Kern was immediately successful. By providing fishermen with a boat and a net, and by offering to buy all the fish they caught, he established the first major industry in north Lincoln County. Simultaneously, he made many men happy by giving hardworking farmers a more enjoyable means of earning a living. The interior of the fish dock is pictured above.

Because a working community grew up around the cannery, there was a need for an official town designation. Consequently, Kernville was established at the cannery in 1896, becoming the first town in north Lincoln County. Daniel's brother John became the first Kernville postmaster that same year. The cannery was sold to Sam Elmore in 1907 and was thenceforth known as the Elmore Cannery, seen here from the Siletz River.

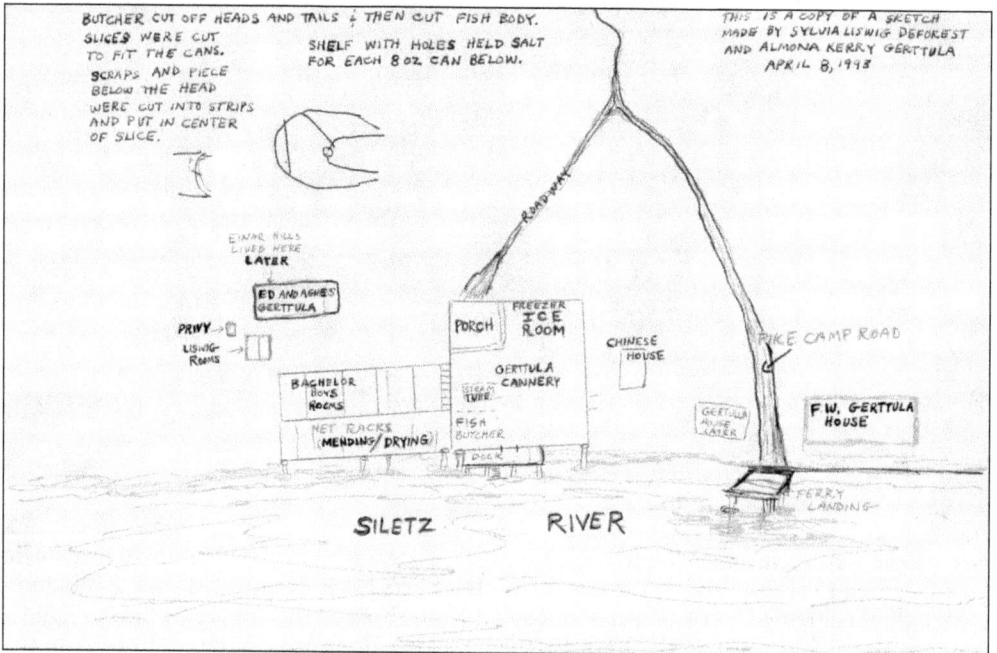

Later the cannery changed hands again. It became the Gerttula Cannery, owned and operated by Ben Gerttula. This sketch drawn by Almona Kerry Gerttula and Sylvia Liswig Deforest illustrates how the cannery buildings were laid out. Note the "Chinese House" used by the Chinese workers who canned the fish. The Chinese cannery workers never became part of the larger community and were soon replaced by local workers.

36

During World War I, a sawmill was erected on the south side of the Siletz River. This location was known as Millport-Kernville. The new town did well until the mill closed and people followed the jobs to new locations. This photograph shows Millport-Kernville after it became a ghost town. Today there are no traces of this once thriving community.

After the war, the town and post office moved back to the north bank of the Siletz River to a new location near a place called Rocky Point, close to present-day Highway 101. The Kernville Store, located just east of the bridge, provided much of what was needed for daily life on the river. The interior of the store is seen in this c. 1935 photograph.

During the 1930s, 1940s, and 1950s, Kernville boomed. Automobile travelers who were headed south had to pass through the town to cross the old Kernville Bridge. That route brought business to Kernville merchants. In later years, Ed Gerttula's Siletz Boat Works, seen here from the Siletz River, was located in Kernville, as well as Killip's Cottages and other river-related businesses.

When the steel girder drawbridge that spanned the Siletz River was completed in November 1926, it provided the last link in the highway between the Columbia River and Yaquina Bay. The drawbridge is seen here at its original location next to the Kernville Store. The old drawbridge was replaced in 1971 with a much higher, much stronger steel bridge, located about 800 feet downstream from the old bridge.

Sissie and Jakie Johnson Jr., seen here in a formal portrait, were Taft's first residents. As Siletz Indians, they were allotted 160 acres along Siletz Bay when reservation lands were opened to white settlement. Settlers to the area held the couple in high esteem. They showed newcomers how to cross Siletz Bay at high tide, pulled wagons out of the sand, and performed many other acts of kindness.

John W. Bones erected the first store in Taft. He named the town for Pres. William Howard Taft, who was then the secretary of war. A post office was established in the store on January 22, 1906, with Bones as the first postmaster. The Bones family is seen here outside their first store. Many descendants of the Bones family still live in the Lincoln City vicinity today.

William M. Dodson purchased the Bones's store in 1911. He also functioned as the town's second postmaster from January 12, 1911, to March 11, 1912. Shortly after the purchase, Dodson constructed a new store and used the old one as a warehouse. Dodson's new store, seen here *c.* 1915, became a vital part of Taft and the surrounding area by providing basic necessities not available anywhere else.

Andrew Alinger became Taft's third postmaster in 1912 when the post office was again relocated to a new store. Alinger built the Spring Store, which was named for an underground spring he used to cool his milk. Pictured here are Sadie Rautio and Andrew Alinger outside the Spring Store, still under construction.

When Fred C. Robison came to Taft in the early 1920s, he purchased the Dodson store, became postmaster, and relocated the post office yet again to the Siletz Trading Company on Fifty-first Street and Coast Highway. In later years, Abe Abrams bought the Siletz Trading Company from Joe DeJardin and renamed it Abrams General Store and Grocery. This business was a hub of activity and commerce until 1960.

During the 1930s and 1940s, Taft was the location for a tourist promotion called "The Redhead Roundup." The roundup started as a beauty contest for redheads but became a three-day annual event when it was understood that the idea had much more than local appeal. Soon it gained state and national attention, bringing thousands of people to Taft, as seen in this 1935 photograph of Siletz Bay.

Schooner Creek was named for a schooner that ran aground in Siletz Bay in the mid-1800s. Until the late 1920s, crossing the creek proved challenging. At first, the creek was crossed by horse, horse and wagon, boat, or by just wading across at low tide. A swinging bridge was constructed across Schooner Creek, just east of the road, in 1911. Although it was a scary crossing, especially in bad weather or for anyone carrying something in their hands, the bridge made it possible to walk across the creek without getting wet. Below, from left to right, Ernest Bones, Dovie Odom Hatfield (Gov. Mark Hatfield's mother), and Rosa Abrams are seen crossing the bridge in 1916. The Schooner Creek covered bridge, constructed in 1927, replaced the swinging bridge. The photograph above shows the covered bridge on Coast Highway c. 1930.

Taft businesses developed primarily along two streets, Pacific Avenue, now Fifty-first Street, and the Roosevelt Coast Military Highway, now Highway 101. Shown here are early businesses on Coast Highway looking south. Note the Snug Harbor on the near right, established at this location around 1930 and still a local business today. Other businesses along this street included a roller rink, the Lincoln Theatre, and the Shop, a general merchandise store.

During World War II, although there was an influx of servicemen, development slowed in Taft. The Green Anchor Café became a favorite eatery for both civilian locals and servicemen. Pictured here are the four Kangiser brothers before they were deployed overseas. They all joined the navy and fought in the war. Thankfully, they all returned home safely.

The Pines Hotel Taft, Oregon

Christian 56

The Pines restaurant and hotel, pictured above in the 1940s, was Taft's living room and kitchen during the 1930s and 1940s. Built some time around 1928, it was <u>the</u> place to stay in Taft for more than 25 years. A disastrous fire completely destroyed the building in 1976. The new Pines restaurant, built on its footprint, is a thriving Lincoln City business today.

Right next door to the Pines hotel was the Taft Hamburger Stand and Pee Wee Golf Course. During the 1940s, the golf course hosted Pacific Northwest golfing champion Eddie Hogan for a successful fund-raising event. The food at the Taft Hamburger Stand was just as good as the miniature golf, judging from how eagerly this German shepherd waits for his burger to arrive in this 1942 photograph.

By 1940, the Taft area was in need of a fire hall for its volunteer firefighters. Volunteer firefighters are dedicated men who protect Lincoln City from fire and rescue those in danger. Accustomed to doing whatever was needed, volunteer firemen held a "building bee" on July 19, 1940, seen in the construction photograph above. When they were done, the Taft-Nelscott-Delake (TND) Volunteer Fire Department had a new home. Bob Ballard was the first fire chief, pictured on the far right in the photograph below with the TND Board of Directors and their brand new fire truck. The firehouse became Lincoln City's first city hall building in 1965. In 1994, it was given to the North Lincoln Pioneer Association and has been the home of the North Lincoln County Historical Museum ever since.

When the Port of Newport built the Taft boat dock on the Siletz Bay waterfront in 1928, it quickly became the center of all fishing, boating, and log-hauling activity. The above photograph shows the Taft dock with the famous *Dodeca*, a tugboat that took log rafts over the treacherous Siletz Bay bar to the sea. Russ Bailey constructed a new dock in 1946 that eventually included a restaurant and boat-rental facility. During the years of Russ Bailey's ownership, the dock became even more of a hub for recreational activity on the bay. Bailey is also credited with rescuing 28 people from drowning who were trapped in the dangerous currents of the Siletz bar. The swimmers in the *c.* 1945 photograph below are, from left to right, Vernal McMullen, Augusta Klimke, a Mrs. Klimke, Guida McMullen, and a Miss Klimke.

The first white people to own land in Cutler City were the people for whom the town was named, George and Mary Cutler, seen in this formal portrait around 1898. The Cutlers first moved to Drift Creek, but they thought the land to the east better suited to future development. In 1904, they purchased a large parcel on Siletz Bay from Charlie Depoe, a Siletz Indian allotment holder. In 1913, the Cutlers built a small cabin southwest of where the Bay House is today. They platted the town site and erected a cabin that same year, but shortly thereafter the family moved back to Dallas, Oregon, due to illness. When George Cutler died in 1914, his son, Arthur George Cutler, inherited the property. Arthur kept a summer home in Cutler City and sold building lots during his visits each summer. He was also instrumental in developing the town's infrastructure and assisted the community by donating land for public use.

The Matt Kangas family was one of the first to settle in Cutler City. In 1905, Sissie and Jakie Johnson sold Matt an 80-acre parcel just south of the Cutler's land. However, it was not until 1919 that the family moved to Drift Creek and started a dairy business. The dairy barn, pictured here, was built to accommodate 40 dairy cows and is still a Cutler City landmark today.

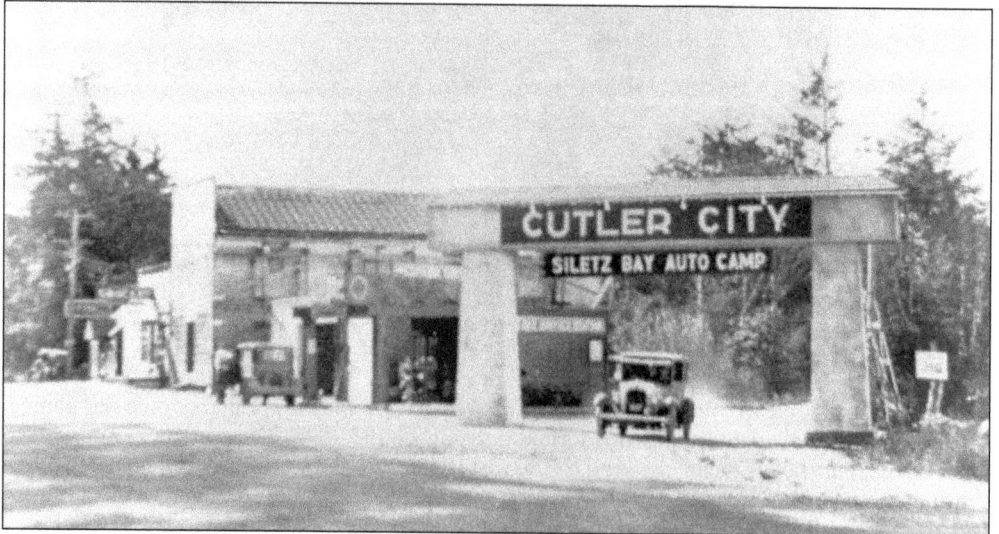

In 1928, the highways that connect this area with the rest of Oregon were completed. The resulting surge in automobile travel brought thousands of visitors to ocean beaches, and auto camping soared in popularity. Cutler City had one of the best, the Siletz Bay Auto Camp. The memorable Cutler City arch, seen here, was built by the auto park to welcome visitors and provide a gateway to the town.

On March 10, 1930, when the town officially became Cutler City, residents greeted the news with jubilation. A post office was established inside Moore's General Store. Norval Moore came to Cutler City in 1929 and started a modest grocery store. By January 1931, he moved to a new location in a new building located on the west side of the highway. Moore's Store was "finished inside in a modern and neat manner, presenting a very fine appearance, favorably comparable to any store of its size anywhere." By the time the business was sold to V. J. LaVigne in 1935, the store was one of the best-known general stores in the county. Moore's Store is seen in this 1940s photograph above. Just north of Moore's Store was C. E. Munker's Richfield Service Station, pictured below with Munker out in front.

New businesses began to spring up in Cutler City in the 1930s, including one that survives today, the Crab Pot. From its earliest days, the Crab Pot was much appreciated for its huge, delectable crab. The original cottage that became the Crab Pot was built about 1922 as a residence. The semi-enclosed porch from which fish were originally sold is seen in this early photograph. The original cottage burned down around 1929 and was replaced in 1930 by Ariel and Alice Thomas. The Bay House, a Cutler City landmark since the mid-1930s, began as the Cutler City Tavern. The tavern had two large stone fireplaces, an outstanding view of Siletz Bay, and excellent food. David Hearing purchased the building and business in 1979, enlarging the dining room and decorating in a "light deco" style.

Cutler City made slow but steady progress during the 1930s, despite the Great Depression. Land sold for approximately $300 for a 50-foot-by-100-foot lot with no improvements. Arthur Cutler offered the lots for $10 down and a payment of $5 a month, an affordable price even when times were hard. This 1930s photograph shows the town's business district along the Coast Highway.

Along with businesses, civic organizations took hold in the 1930s. Cutler City residents began construction on the Cutler City Community Club in 1936. Built on land offered by Arthur Cutler, the community club became the center for all civic and social activity. Groups met to discuss city improvements, celebrate birthdays and holidays, raise funds for charity, and put on community dances and craft festivals. (Courtesy of Lincoln County Historical Society.)

The North Lincoln Rhododendron Society was organized in 1938 to preserve as many wild rhododendrons as possible throughout north Lincoln County. Cutler City, with the most plants, was selected as its "Rhododendron Capital." Rhododendron Days and May Festivals of Beauty were held annually from 1938 to 1941 to celebrate the blooming season. This photograph of an unidentified woman shows the size and abundance of the "rhoddies" in Cutler City.

Cutler City was a small town with little traffic, except on Coast Highway. Accidents like this one did not impede the flow of traffic a bit. However, when Cutler City experienced a housing boom after World War II, traffic increased exponentially both in town and along the highway. Today there is a constant stream of cars traveling the highway.

The area that would become Nelscott remained uninhabited until 1910 when August Wallace took up residence as a homesteader. He built his one-room cabin out of hand-hewn shakes from lumber that washed up on shore from a shipwreck. Wallace was known for his fishing but even more for his practice of stripping naked and swimming out to the distant rocks to collect succulent mussels found there.

Charles P. Nelson, a Cloverdale store owner, brought supplies by boat to Siletz Bay merchants. One day in 1906, he decided to walk home from Taft. About a mile along the beach, he saw a wide opening in the sandstone cliffs that revealed a small, lush valley so beautiful he never forgot it. Early Nelscott is seen in this photograph after the first roads were cleared.

In 1925, Charles P. Nelson and Dr. W. G. Scott set out to find land along the Oregon coast to develop as a beach resort. Nelson recalled the land he had seen on his walk and found that a large parcel was for sale. The two men purchased a tract of 170 acres for $4,000. That land constituted the original town site of Nelscott. When they tried to decide on a name for the town, Nelson's wife, Nannie, seen here between Charles and their son Earl, suggested combining the two last names, and the town was christened Nelscott Beach. In 1929, the name was shortened to Nelscott when the first post office was established, and Charles Nelson became the first postmaster. The Nelscott Land Company was formed in 1925. Below, Charles Nelson stands in front of the post office.

Frank Hallock built the Nelscott Cash Store in the spring of 1927. The store was the heart of the town and included a general store, the first offices of the Nelscott Land Company, a bus depot, a restaurant, a beauty parlor, and, by 1929, the post office. During rush hour and on busy Saturdays, the store needed six clerks. Anna Cushing operated the restaurant, famous for its home cooking and generous portions. The Nelscott Auto Park Service Station, seen at the far left below, was also an integral part of the Nelscott community. Before 1925, few cars were seen on the coast. However, once people started arriving in their automobiles, they required services to get them on the road again. Both of these photographs show the Nelscott Store c. 1929.

The Nelscott Land Company began by selling lots for vacation homes. Dr. W. G. Scott promoted the development in Portland while the Nelsons entertained prospective buyers during the summers and on weekends with beach games, bonfires, and airplane rides. In this photograph are an unidentified pilot and passenger with one of the planes that took off and landed on the Nelscott beach. The cost was 25¢ per ride.

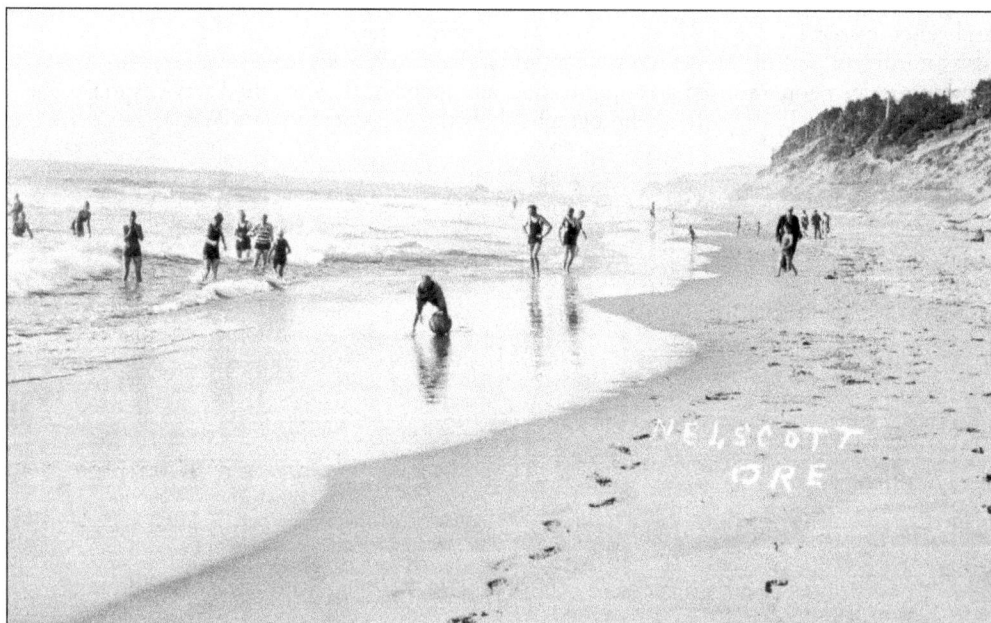

Nelscott experienced a tremendous growth spurt from the late 1920s through the 1930s. Visitors from Portland and the Willamette Valley spent summers and weekends on the Nelscott beach swimming and enjoying the surf and sand, as seen in this early 1930 photograph. When Nelscott first became a town in 1925, the population numbered only three, all members of the Burdick family. By 1950, there were more than 400 residents.

In the spring of 1932, the Nelsons moved their business to a new building south of the store and the "Nelscott Strip" was born. Charles's son Earl opened the Lincoln Book Shop and Lending Library, seen in this photograph, on the "strip" in 1937. Earl was a true intellectual. Because of an early childhood illness, he developed a quiet lifestyle that revolved around books, movies, and art. His personal collection of books was once described as "one of the nation's finest libraries." The lending library started with a few shelves in the office of the Taft-Nelscott Water District but grew until it served the whole community. For many years, Earl's bookshop was a center for art and culture in the community. Below, this 1947 interior photograph of the bookshop shows Earl downstairs, browsing through a book.

When the popularity of auto camping soared during the early 1920s, coastal towns established auto parks to accommodate travelers. George and Anna Cushing started the Nelscott Auto Park in 1927, seen here from an unpaved Coast Highway. They felled and burned trees, cleared brush, and built a campground. The auto park consisted of cottages, tent houses, auto campsites, a service station, and a homey Community Kitchen.

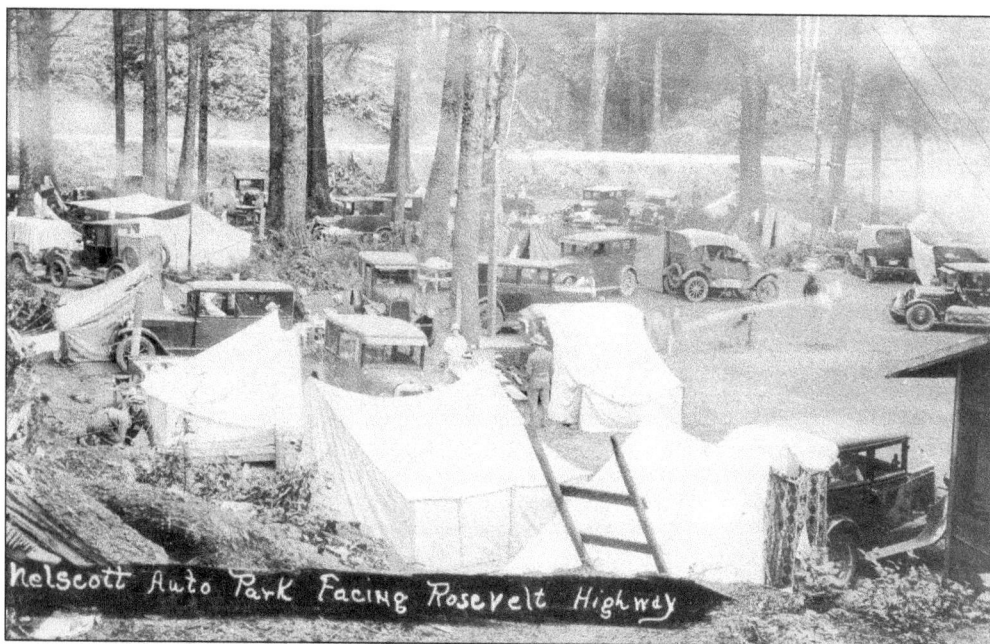

At first, auto park guests slept in their cars or set up a tent they carried in the trunk. Some ingenious souls attached homemade awnings directly to their vehicle to provide shelter, as seen in this 1929 photograph. By the 1930s, there were sometimes as many as 100 tents and autos in the campground. A "deluxe" campsite cost 75¢ a night, while a one-bed cottage rented for $1.

58

The auto park's Community Kitchen gave locals a place to gather for community meetings and provided a comfortable indoor place to eat for campers. Church services were held there, as well as piano recitals and sing-alongs. This 1935 photograph shows the Community Kitchen fireplace, built out of beach rock and typical of home and cottage fireplaces built in the area throughout the 1930s and 1940s by Frank Mann.

This c. 1937 photograph shows Nelscott thriving, due in part to the influence of Earl Nelson. Even before he established the library, he encouraged Oregon authors to vacation in Nelscott. Ben Hur Lampman wrote many of his editorials and short stories at his summer home in Nelscott, called the "Gray Hackle." From 1937 to 1948, more than 200 authors, some of them nationally and internationally known, visited the town.

The Chapel by the Sea was established by the Presbyterians of Oregon for use by all cooperating denominations. Before a church was built, the community held church meetings under the trees in the auto park, as seen in this c. 1934 photograph above. Construction on a church building was started in September 1936 on 13 acres of land donated by Charles Nelson. The church was dedicated on June 13, 1937, with Dr. Alfred M. Williams acting as the first pastor. The church bell, brought from the disbanded McCoy Presbyterian Church in Polk County, was presented to the chapel by the Reverend Joseph Y. Stewart of Albany. Maude Wanker designed the beautiful memorial window in the church in honor of Dr. Williams. The chapel building was a Nelscott landmark until 2007.

On Your Vacation Trail – WINTER and SUMMER

MEET US AT
- The Chapel-by-the-Sea
- The Manse Guest House
- The Chapel Woods
  (New 10-acre gift to be developed) —

The Williamses
NELSCOTT, Oregon

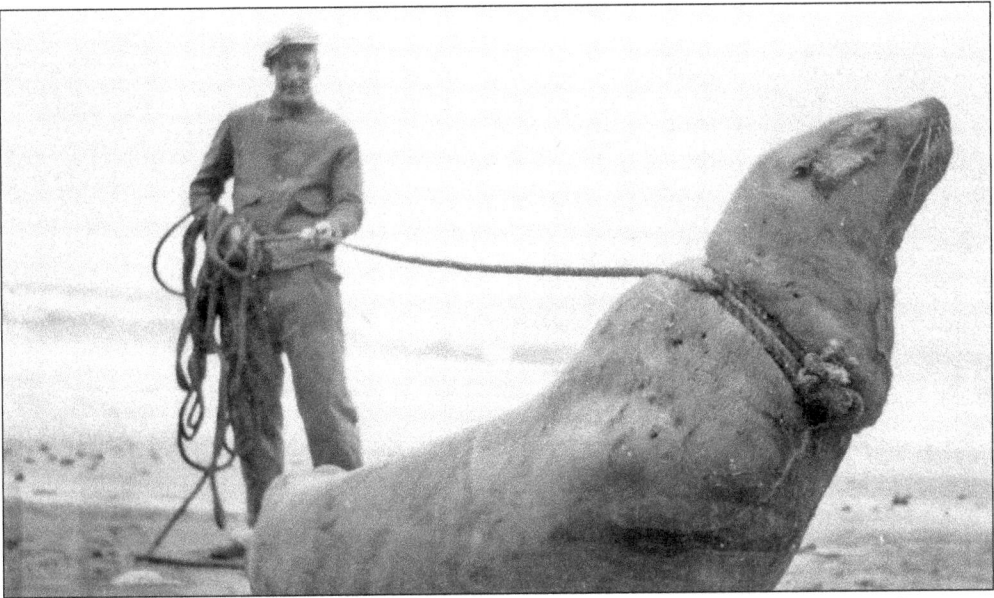

Nelscott made the front page of the *Oregonian* during the last week of March 1933, when a sea lion visited and took up residence. Christened "Joe the Sea Lion," he climbed over picket fences with the greatest of ease, careful not to crush flowers or break flowerpots. He made numerous attempts to enter houses and loved to be bathed with a garden hose or have his back scratched with a broom.

This photograph shows how a rare snowstorm covered Nelscott homes and the adjacent beach with snow during the late 1940s. Because onshore breezes are usually warm, snow seldom stays on the ground at the coast for more than a few minutes. Nelscott development is also illustrated in this street scene where houses, apartments, and cottages line the beach and fill much of the open space that had been vacant two decades earlier.

The war years were some of the most eventful years in Nelscott's history. Men from nearly every state in the Union were stationed there. The first year, the Army Signal Corps quartered at the former Nelscott Auto Park. The U.S. Coast Guard replaced them the following year. Joe Katurna, a member of the coast guard, watches a blimp patrol the shoreline for Japanese submarines in this 1943 photograph.

With the influx of soldiers at the beginning of World War II, the population soared in Nelscott. But while many servicemen and women came to the area, others left to serve in the war. Frank N. Parent flew the flag in this photograph of the Nelscott beach access for his daughter Peggy (Lutz) every day she served away from home as a U. S. Navy Wave.

The first post office in Delake, seen in this 1924 photograph above, was established once the town had an official name. The origin of the name Delake has two versions. In one, the name was derived from the accent of Finnish homesteaders, who said, "I'm going to *de* lake." In another, the *d* and *e* constitute a French word meaning "by," hence the area "by the lake" became Delake.

Delake was once known as "Camp Roosevelt," named by early homesteader Alvin W. Thorpe. His brother, Harry Thorpe, named his homestead land "Roosevelt by the Sea." Both men named the area for Pres. Theodore Roosevelt. This photograph shows the Roosevelt Coast Military Highway, also named for the popular president, with two of the first cars to use the road.

63

The Delake Commercial Club was the center of all the early Delake community activities. The Delake Chamber of Commerce held its meetings there, and residents gathered for celebrations and meetings of all kinds. This 1928 photograph shows the community gathered at the Commercial Club for a big, area-wide parade celebrating the completion of the Salmon River Highway.

The Lincoln County Art Center and Gallery by the Sea was started by Maude Wanker and Ruth Grover, two nationally known artists, at the Delake Community House, seen here. With the help of other artists, they made the center one of the most important art galleries on the Pacific coast. Grover and Wanker taught art at the center and held exhibitions that included art by prominent artists and students.

Students who attended classes at the Lincoln County Art Center had the opportunity to have some of the well-known residents of the county as models. Eleanor Kramer, of Eleanor's Undertow restaurant, was painted twice. Classes were held in the winter, and heat for the building came from a potbellied stove. Students and models complained that the room was cold unless one sat close to the stove.

Delake Elementary School, seen here c. 1930, was built at its present location in 1927 to accommodate a rapidly growing population. By September 1930, it still had only two finished classrooms and no restrooms, just two wooden "privies" out back. The two schoolrooms housed four grades each. The historic school building on Sixth Street and Highway 101 is occupied today by the Lincoln City Cultural Center.

In the late 1940s and early 1950s, Delake had a thriving business district. The photograph above shows a street scene looking north on Coast Highway, just about where the Delake Wayside is today. On the right is the Lighthouse Mobil Station, once a distinctive landmark in Delake. On the left is the Point of View Tavern, located where the D Sands Motel now stands. Not visible across from the Lighthouse Mobil Station and behind the tavern is the Delake Aquarium, seen in the photograph below. Aquariums of this kind, which dotted the coast, were hugely popular with visitors during the 1930s and 1940s. Exhibits included seals, sea lions, otters, and octopi, as well as a variety of sea and tide-pool life.

Two Delake landmarks that exist today in new incarnations are the Canyon Drive Apartments and the Seven Gables Cottages. The Canyon Drive Apartments (pictured above) were located adjacent to the Delake Beach access near Canyon Drive Park. Residents built a rock wall and a paved drive along Canyon Drive in the 1940s. They wanted to aid the war effort by making it possible for military cars and trucks to drive onto the beach. In the 1980s, the city of Lincoln City installed a seawall of precast concrete blocks along the oceanfront edge and paved a parking area at the same access point. The Seven Gables Cottages (pictured below) were built around 1928. They were supposed to be the Eleven Gables Cottages, but the builder ran out of money. In 1969, the cottages were converted to retail shops and are still in use today.

The shore along the D River, on the east side of the highway, was once a popular recreation spot. Children swam and took lessons in the slightly salty, slightly fresh water of the river, safely out of the way of "sneaker" waves. People also fished there, rented canoes and motorboats, and water-skied to the lake. In this 1959 photograph, children swim near Calkins Craft, a Delake boatbuilding business.

The A-frame building in this photograph is the Anchorage, a drive-in restaurant for boats, that was owned and operated by Bert and Mary Koning. The Konings loved teenagers and furnished the restaurant with casual tables, benches, and a jukebox filled with popular music. Mary cooked "space burgers" for the kids, made with a special meat mixture stuffed inside grilled bread or corn tortillas shaped like a space ship.

The D River, which runs through the center of Delake, marks the center of Lincoln City as well. Legend has it that the river was a favorite spot for Native Americans to catch salmon long before white settlers came to know it. According to Earl Nelson, a Native American battle was fought there in 1853. The battle broke out over fishing rights when a local Yaquina tribe encountered some Rogue River Indians clubbing salmon and throwing them on shore as they made their way up the river. The D River has been known by various names in the past, including the "outlet," since it is where Devils Lake empties into the ocean. A contest to officially name the river was conducted in 1940. Today the river is known as the shortest river in the world with the shortest name.

Oceanlake was once known as "Devils Lake Park," named by Herbert Rexroad and Edgar Hoyt, two men who bought 82 acres of land in what became the main business district of the town. Seen in this 1927 photograph of the property are, from left to right, William Herbert Rexroad, Edna Iola King Rexroad, and William King, Edna's father.

The Rexroads built the first house in the area in 1924 and went on to construct the first store. The Devils Lake Park Campground was built next. The campground included cabins, not seen in this c. 1930 photograph, and accommodated up to 300 campers.

Before Oceanlake had a post office and an official name, it was also called "Raymond," named for the famous "singing priest of Siletz," Fr. Charles Raymond. Father Raymond acquired considerable property for a church that would serve both Native Americans and white settlers. St. Augustine Catholic Church was built by Father Raymond in 1924 at its current location in the small building pictured here.

In 1926, a post office was established in Oceanlake, seen here with A. C. Deuel, the first postmaster on the far left. Mrs. H. E. Warren is credited with naming the town by saying, "it lies between the ocean and the lake." It was a unique name; there were Oceansides, Lakesides, and Sealakes but only one postal name of Oceanlake in the United States.

In the late 1920s and early 1930s, Oceanlake's business district along the highway grew rapidly. Automobile service stations began to spring up, as well as stores and even a dance hall to serve residents and visitors. The Oceanlake Dance Hall, seen on the near right of this 1920s street scene, was a local hot spot for more than two decades.

The Oceanlake Dance Hall was also a place for the community to gather for photographs and civic meetings, as well as for dancing. This 1929 photograph in front of the dance hall shows a large group of well-dressed residents gathered for a Fourth of July parade. Note the Boy Scout troop from Toledo on the steps out front, ready to march in the parade.

Dancing was usually informal at the dance hall. Couples even brought their young children, who were allowed to dance, play, or fall asleep on the floor. Special gala events like the Devils Lake Regatta Ball were different. This interior photograph shows ladies in gowns and men in formal dress at the ball. People dressed in all their finery to see and be seen on these important social occasions.

Agate collecting and tide-pool watching have always been favorite activities on Oceanlake beaches. Beach agates were plentiful in those days. This c. 1932 photograph shows people enjoying the beach at low tide, when sea urchins and sea stars can be seen and touched in the pools of water created by rocks along the shore. At high tide, these rocks are sometimes completely covered by sand and water.

WHITES COTTAGES - OCEANLAKE, ORE.   CHANDLE

According to their journals, Rev. Jason and Anna Maria Lee, Mr. and Mrs. Cyrus Shepard, and their guide, Joseph Gervais, came to the Oceanlake area for a honeymoon trip in August 1837. They set up camp in a grove of trees near the ocean, just as tourists did 100 years later. Although getting here on horseback was not easy, the couples reported a pleasant and healthful stay, enjoying many seafood dinners cooked on an open fire. Later-day tourists were likely to stay at either the Warrens Cottages or Mrs. White's Cottages. White's Addition to Oceanlake, a large section of property along the oceanfront, is where a Mrs. White built some of the earliest rental cottages, pictured above bordering Fifteen Street, then known as Raymond Avenue. Warrens Cottages catered to hunters and fishermen, as seen in the photograph below c. 1938.

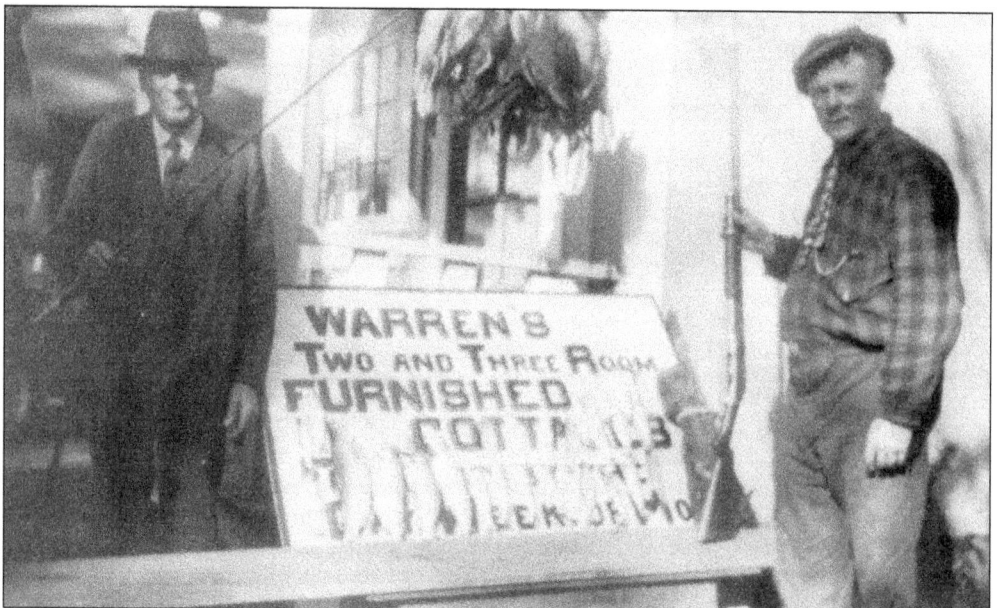

WARREN'S
TWO AND THREE ROOM
FURNISHED
COTTAGES

The Lakeside Theatre opened in June 1937 with a Jean Harlow movie; admission was a whopping 35¢. William McKevitt owned the 270-seat movie house. After World War II, William's son Robert took over the operation and initiated the first major renovation. In 1979, the theater closed but was reopened by Judy Mace in 1982. Keith and Betsy Altomare have owned the theater, now named the Bijou, since 1996.

The Iris N Ranch, seen here, was located on Northeast Twenty-fourth Street near where St. James Episcopal church is today. The name came from Iris Nanos, the daughter of the Nanos family, who owned the property before 1953. In that year, the property was sold, and the house was converted into a small hospital with 10 beds, a surgery, a laboratory, and a delivery room. In the late 1950s, it became a convalescent hospital.

The beach along Oceanlake's shoreline is one of the best places to surf fish on the Oregon coast. Surf fishing is challenging and dangerous, as seen in this photograph around 1950. High surf and rogue waves cause a fisherman or fisherwoman to engage the ocean in a constant dance of approach and retreat, all the while trying to reel in a fighting fish. Consequently, surf fishing is seldom seen today.

During the 1940s and 1950s, people parked their cars right on the hard-packed beach sand. Visitors sometimes parked close to the water when the tide was out, thinking they were in a safe spot. However, if they left their cars and the tide changed, they sometimes returned to discover their car stuck in the sand and oncoming waves. The cars in this c. 1940 photograph are well back from the surf.

Surftides on the Beach originally opened as the Surf Tide Apartments in the Oceanlake area once known as Braemar Beach. Rented by the week or by the month, these upscale apartments had a wonderful ocean view. Later, when the property was sold and renovated, the name was changed to Surftides. Apartments were still rented, as well as hotel rooms and suites. By the 1950s, Surftides had a modern look, as seen in the above photograph of the glass-enclosed, all-year swimming pool. Amenities at Surftides also included a large recreation room, a snack bar, and riding stables. Horseback riding on the beach was common during the 1950s. Guests shown at right "horsing around" are obviously enjoying their stay. The beach was even lit at night to insure guests a 24-hour view of the Pacific Ocean.

The word "wecoma," found in John Gill's *Dictionary of Chinook Jargon*, means "sea" or "big waters." One local legend tells that when inland Native Americans first sighted the ocean, they exclaimed, "Wecoma!," meaning "Welcome big waters." Justice of the peace Frank Holmes is credited with naming the town Wecoma because of this legend. This late 1940s photograph shows Wecoma businesses along the west side of Coast Highway.

Wecoma's northern limits extended to Roads End where ocean caves once stood at the base of Cascade Head. Although most of the caves on the beach have eroded over time, beachcombers can still access a few when the tide is very low. The Ocean Caves Grocery Store, shown here in this *c.* 1950 photograph, now houses the Rockfish Bakery, Days Catch Collectibles, and Safari Town Surf Shop.

The Dorchester House, now on the National Register of Historic Places, was Wecoma's most recognizable building. Construction began on the Dorchester House in 1929, but the Depression delayed its opening until July 1935. Rowe Kennedy designed the Colonial-style building for owner/builder Charles Walker. Walker wanted to create a hotel reminiscent of an English country inn, complete with English-style amenities, ambiance, and hospitality.

During its early years, the Dorchester House was the only "fancy" hotel in the area. The popularity of the establishment and increasing motor traffic encouraged Charles Walker to enlarge the building. He added another gable, more rooms on the upper level, and a lobby with office space on the first floor. A spectacular ocean view is seen from one of the second-floor guest rooms in this c. 1938 photograph.

Guests at the Dorchester House enjoyed crackling fires in the lobby's stone fireplace, constructed from river and ocean rocks hand selected by mason Frank Mann. He built the fireplace one foot at a time, allowing each foot of mortar and stone to dry for up to five days before continuing his work. The original fireplace can still be seen in the living room of the Dorchester House today.

The Dorchester House once advertised with a freestanding sign beside the highway, adorned with a boar's head in the tradition of the English inns that inspired its designer. This advertisement shows the cost of a fine hotel room on the Oregon coast during the 1930s and 1940s. The Dorchester House is now an elegant retirement home for active seniors.

When Lacey's Doll Museum opened in 1951, it quickly became Wecoma's favorite tourist attraction. Helen Lacey, an avid doll collector, loved to see all of her dolls displayed. Over the years, her collection grew to more than 4,000 antique dolls, one of the largest in the country. More than 2,000 dolls and other collectibles, seen in this photograph, were on exhibit at the museum for more than 30 years.

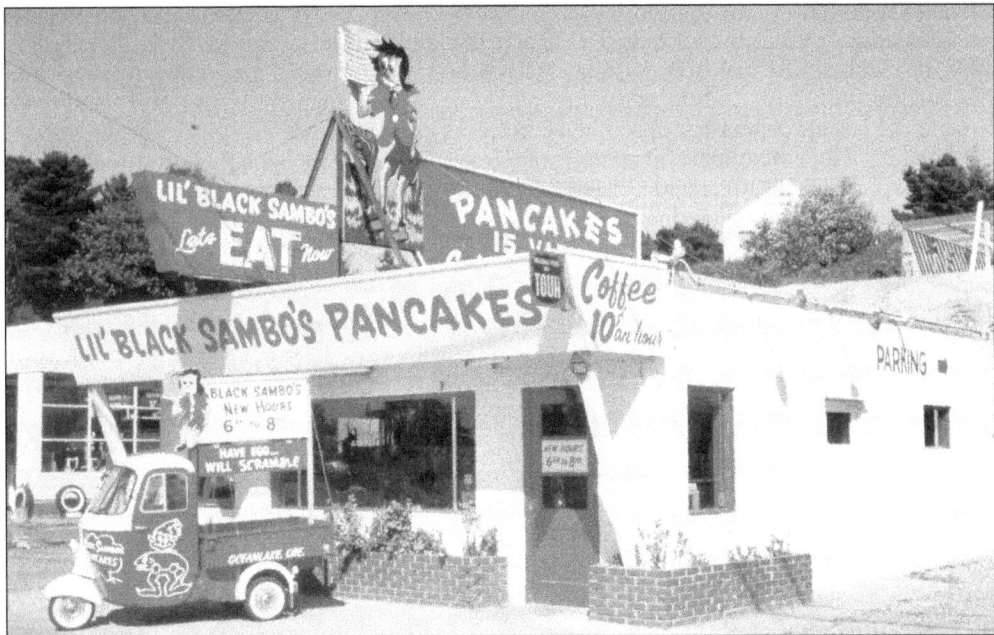

Lil' Black Sambos, another memorable Wecoma business, is pictured in this c. 1955 photograph. When the original building burned down in 2002, local residents were devastated. However, the popular restaurant was quickly replaced by Lil Sambos, built on the footprint of the original building in 2003. Sambos still serves pancakes and has great ambiance, but it no longer has the little three-wheel delivery vehicle seen in this photograph.

Mr and Mrs O. M. Dodson — Rose Lodge Oregon

Rose Covered Entrance in Summer

ROSE LODGE P.O.

Oliver Dodson came to the coast in 1898 from Dallas, Oregon, on the advice of area homesteader Jim Crowley. In 1907, Dodson acquired a 120-acre homestead near the Salmon River. By February 1908, he had built the first store on Salmon River Road and started a post office in the back of the building with Julia Dodson as the first postmistress. Julia named the post office and town Rose Lodge because it was descriptive of the bower of climbing roses that grew over the front of the building. There were some 50 varieties of roses, sent to Julia by her father. In this delightful collage of photographs, Julia and Oliver Dodson, the original Rose Lodge post office and store, and the Dodson children standing under the roses are all pictured.

The Rose Lodge Store and Post Office was originally located across the highway, southeast of its present location. Pictured here are, from left to right, (seated) Albert Hunt, Henry Gregory, and Pat Gregory; (standing in the doorway) Viola and Clara Hunt. The dog, Larry Shane, helped herd cows. Once, when his master was ill, Larry Shane brought the herd across the highway and into the barn all on his own.

Rose Lodge had a grade school, a high school, and a grange. The grange was used as a dance hall as well as for events like Easter egg hunts. The Rose Lodge Grade School interior is shown here around 1948. A popular teacher, a Mrs. Boggey (far right), is seen here among her smiling students. Former students fondly remember the school for its great teachers, open school grounds, and after-school baseball games.

In 1919, Henry and Rita Gregory bought the Rose Lodge property originally owned by the Dodsons from Henry and Millie Deakins. The land included the original 120-acre homestead but not the store. The Deakins eventually purchased the Rose Lodge Store and Post Office in 1935. Henry's son Pat and his wife, Gladys, ran both operations. In 1937, the building that housed the store and post office burned and a new building replaced it, but on the other side of the highway. The building and business are still there today. The photograph above shows the Gregory home after it was relocated in 1937. Below, Mark and Ruth Powell sit beside a beautiful rock wall and garden built by Pat and Gladys, just off North Bank Road, with Highway 18 in the background.

Ernestine Baller is seen here *c.* 1940 near the concrete bridge that spans Slick Rock Creek on Highway 18. Slick Rock Creek, which flows from the southeast hills in Rose Lodge, converges at this point with the Salmon River. This is also the location of a deep swimming hole, a favorite spot for local residents to picnic and swim from the 1930s to today.

Rose Lodge provided a gateway to north Lincoln County from points east via Highway 18. This covered bridge, called the "old red bridge," spanned the Salmon River on North Bank Road. Built in 1910, this photograph shows the bridge in its last days after more than 60 years of use. The bridge was completely taken out when a storm brought large trees and debris hurtling downstream in the 1970s.

North Lincoln County's third post office was established in Otis on April 24, 1900, at Archibald Samuel Thompson's home. Thompson named the town Otis in honor of his brother's son, Otis Thompson. Mel Burton, a pioneer mail carrier, is pictured here outside the first Otis Post Office. His delivery route took him from Rose Lodge to Kernville. Burton was admired and liked by all who knew him.

Settlers and homesteaders reached coastal towns by traveling along the Old Indian Trail. The trail became a military road, then the market road seen in this photograph, and finally in 1927, it became the Salmon River Highway. This road played an important role in the history of Lincoln County because it connected the coast with cities in the Willamette Valley that could provide the supplies and equipment necessary for development.

The Otis Café, pictured here, is one of the best-known restaurants on the coast. Tourists have stopped for breakfast at the café for decades as they continued on their travels. The Otis Café and gas station are located at Otis Junction, the point where the Salmon River Highway meets the old, scenic Highway 101. The present-day Otis Post Office is just next door to the café.

This photograph shows Otis residents (from left to right) Bill and Lexie (Fraser) Griswold and Lexie's brother Del Fraser. They are pictured in front of the Mobile station at Otis Junction, just across old Highway 101 from the Richfield service station. Bill and his brother Guy built the Mobile station, originally a wooden building. The wooden structure was later replaced with a cement block building, which is still in use today.

Old scenic Highway 101 is seen in these rare photographs, along with the covered bridge that once spanned the Salmon River in Otis. Highway 101 originally took this winding route through dense woods. Although longer than the present route, the scenic course bypassed the steep grade over Cascade Head. Not until 1960 was a direct route over Cascade Head completed and paved. The Otis Grade School, on the northwest side of the bridge, is not visible in this photograph. The school building is now the home of the Otis Fire Department. The photograph below shows a group gathered around a fire truck in the early 1950s. The group is getting ready for a parade that will wind through the neighboring coastal towns in celebration of the new fire truck's arrival.

The Talbot Cottages, located 300 yards south of Otis Junction, were among the few accommodations that catered to fishermen and river lovers rather than ocean lovers. Thompson's Landing, located nearby, rented fishing boats and sold fishing tackle and bait. The Otis Store, owned by Gayton Phelps, sold supplies and groceries to visiting sportsmen as well as local residents.

Just down the road, next door to the service station at Otis Junction, was Hall's Seafood. Hall's sold souvenirs and curios as well as crab, oysters, and fresh fish. At one time, the business included a small zoo that had a monkey, two black bears, and a dubious coyote that some people said was really a dog.

The name Neotsu came from a book of Native American lore. A group of Devils Lake women read the book and came across the word *neotsu*, meaning "lake by the ocean." They decided that the name was a perfect fit for the town. The Neotsu of yesteryear was characterized by open fern hills, as seen in both of these early photographs, not covered with alders and homes as it is today. Resident Native Americans annually burned off the ground cover in February when there was almost two weeks of dry weather. The cleared hillsides made it easier to ride horses into the hills when hunting, while lower lands were kept as grassy pastures. Some residents claim remnants of the military road built by Phil Sheridan's men in 1850 can still be seen in Neotsu today.

Credit for much of the early progress in the Neotsu area must go to Bud Jones, who opened and developed the present town site in 1925. Before that time, there were a few cabins on the lake, a school, a post office, and not much else. This photograph shows people feeding the beautiful swans that once inhabited Devils Lake.

Neotsu was always a bedroom community, and it never had much of a business presence. An exception was the Devils Lake Hotel, located in Neotsu on the north end of Devils Lake. The hotel had a café downstairs, and upstairs were guest rooms that had lovely views of the lake. The hotel was also the official headquarters for the Devils Lake Regatta, an important tourism promotion involving the entire town.

The Ocean Air Speedway, located in Neotsu at the north end of East Devils Lake Road, was a track of hard-packed dirt. The owner had a man working for her, "a real promoter from California who talked some guys from Portland into coming down to race hardtops." Unfortunately, none of the racers made much money. Although the racers paid nothing to participate, they came from far away cities and expected to win big. Tickets were sold to spectators, but with the owner and the promoter getting a percentage of the profits from the gate, there was only about $100 to divide among the winners. Even the "big winner" received only $20. Racers soon went elsewhere, following the lure of big cash prizes. The quarter-mile racetrack was in operation during the summer of 1953.

Neotsu hugs the shore of Devils Lake. Consequently, many Neotsu residents have homes on the water that include boat ramps. People who enjoy water-related activities, such as canoeing, water-skiing, and fishing, are likely to choose Neotsu as their home. Views of the water and the surrounding mountains can be seen from almost any spot in Neotsu. The town is just far enough away from the ocean mist to be called "sunny Neotsu" by area residents. Neotsu also has the distinction of being located right on the 45th parallel, halfway between the equator and the North Pole. Stan Allyn, a well-known excursion fishing boat captain and the owner of the *Kingfisher*, took this 1953 photograph of his daughters Linda and Beverly Allyn. Stan Allyn operated the business out of Depoe Bay from 1932 to 1992. (Courtesy of Lincoln County Historical Society.)

The town of Lincoln Beach is located in a beautiful living forest of cedar and rhododendron. Lincoln Beach was so named by George Betts, the first postmaster, because it is a beach town in Lincoln County. Betts established a post office in Lincoln Beach on May 22, 1933. As with most coastal towns, the beach was the town's main attraction, and beachcombing was a favorite activity of residents and tourists alike. The above photograph of a family with its Japanese glass float collection gives one an idea of the abundance of floats that washed ashore in Lincoln Beach during the 1930s and 1940s. Even though the ocean sometimes offered up good things, it was still a constant source of danger, especially for fishermen. Below is the *Unga*, a fishing boat, run aground in Lincoln Beach after a bad storm.

Samuel Zarate, a classically trained musician and composer, earned an international reputation for his guitar and violin playing. When Samuel met and married Paquita, they became a musical team, performing across Europe, the Far East, India, and Australia. In 1959, they opened a cultural center in Lincoln Beach, where they offered piano, guitar, and flute lessons. In 1962, they purchased a home called Trails End on six acres of land in Lincoln Beach. Next to their house sat two life-sized, white, cement oxen pulling a covered wagon, seen below. These two oxen were the most visible landmarks in Lincoln Beach for many years.

As tourism became the primary economic base in north Lincoln County, more residents and business owners saw the value in advertising what coastal beaches had to offer. Events like the Salmon Derby were promoted throughout Oregon. This 1952 photograph of a professional model shows one of the many tourist promotions in Lincoln Beach. Note the Japanese mine covered in barnacles that washed up in Lincoln Beach after the war.

Lincoln Beach was always a desirable place to live a quiet life. Although slow to develop a business district, its residential district grew steadily during the 1930s and 1940s. Civic groups formed to meet the needs of the community. This photograph shows the large turnout for a Lincoln Beach Lions Club banquet in the 1940s.

96

The Sijota family first settled the area that became Gleneden Beach. Since this family of Polish immigrants was the area's only residents, the town was originally known as Sijota. The area was remote, even for coastal towns, as seen in this photograph looking south from the main road. Because schools of the day were far from the Sijota homestead, Mary Sijota started a school in her home.

The Sijotas were a popular, hardworking family. The children, pictured here when they were teenagers, were expected to work as hard as the adults both before and after they attended school. The Sijota girls were said to have been as strong as the boys, able to easily heft and carry large sacks of grain.

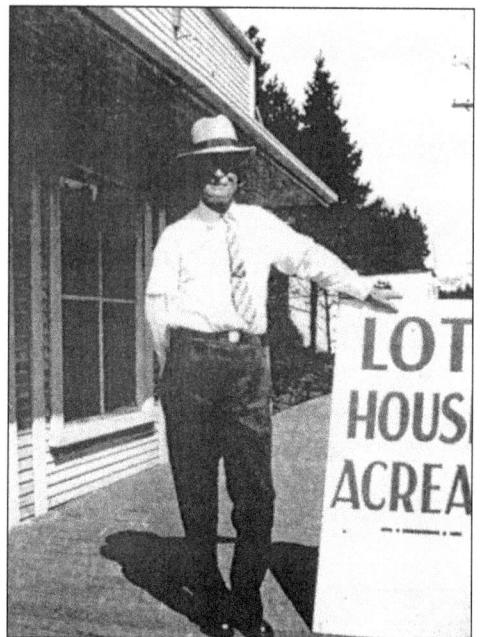

In the mid-1920s, Mr. and Mrs. William F. Cary, seen in these 1930 photographs above, purchased a large parcel of land from the Sijotas. They had two daughters, Glen and Phyllis. The Carys formed the Siletz Investment Company for the purpose of selling residential and vacation home lots. They chose the name "Gleneden" for the developing town by combining the name of their daughter Glen with the word "Eden," suggestive of paradise. "Beach" was added later for advertising purposes. In 1927, the town included 225 lots, a water department, and a post office, but the Coast Highway was not yet surfaced, and there was no bridge over the Siletz River, so the town was still hard to reach. The round house seen in the photograph below was one of the more unusual homes in Gleneden Beach.

The Cary family continued to be active in the development of Gleneden Beach. When a post office was established in 1927, William Cary became the first postmaster. Emily Sijota, a postmistress for more than 20 years, succeeded him. The Gleneden Cottages (pictured here), a grocery store, gas stations, an auto court, a variety store, and a concrete plant were all part of the town of Gleneden Beach.

The Pilot Wheel Cottages were originally built to accommodate summer visitors. Later they were rented by the week, then by the month, and finally were sold as residences. Today a few of the cottages remain, like the lovely one in this 1947 photograph. Some of the original brick fireplaces still stand among the trees, with no sign of the cottages they warmed.

The Logs was a beautiful dance hall, bar, and restaurant named for the fir logs from which it was constructed. It opened in 1938 and quickly became a local hot spot. The music was local and always good. At one end of the large, open hall was a huge rock fireplace that provided ample heat for the diners. Beautiful hardwood floors were ideal for dancing. The bar was so busy it took two bartenders and four waitresses to handle the business on an average night. Alcohol use by some of the young men meant the dances were sometimes prematurely ended when fights broke out. The restaurant was a popular place for formal banquets and other community events. This c. 1940 photograph below shows the Logs on the Coast Highway during its heyday. The Logs burned to the ground in 1974.

The origin of the name Depoe Bay comes from Native American allotment holders Charles, William, and Matilda Depoe, and from the bay, which forms the town's most dramatic geological feature. Charles, or Charlie as he was better known, is seen here in full regalia in the 1930s. Many Native Americans adopted or were given English names by the settlers who could not pronounce their Indian names. Charlie was called "Depot Charlie" because of his diligence in making sure supplies intended for the Siletz Reservation were not "lost" en route. Depot, gentrified to Depoe, was used by Charlie on government documents, and it was by this name that he became widely known. Charlie Depoe and his family were held in high esteem by homesteaders, who adopted the name for the town when they opened a post office in 1928.

The heirs of Charlie Depoe sold their land to Lee Williams. The Sunset Investment Company purchased the parcel from Williams in 1926 for $10,000, dividing it into building lots that sold for $100 each. Although the company's interest was primarily commercial, it sponsored community events to thank the people and businesses of Depoe Bay. Visible in this 1928 photograph are the holdings of the Sunset Investment Company before development.

In this early Depoe Bay photograph is Arch Rock with its crown of wind-blown spruce trees, once a distinctive natural feature of Depoe Bay. Unfortunately, Arch Rock collapsed into the sea many years ago. Like so many basalt rock formations, it was eroded by the constant pounding of ocean waves.

102

The Spouting Horn, Depoe Bay, Ore. Chandler Photo

The Spouting Horn, seen in these photographs, is Depoe Bay's most popular natural attraction. A "spouting horn" occurs when surging waves roll underneath a rock formation. The force of the wave pushes water up through a small opening at the surface where it shoots into the air. Every wave produces another spray, sometimes shooting saltwater 300 feet into the air. Depoe Bay's Spouting Horn is especially exciting at sunset when the spray becomes incandescent with brilliant rainbow colors. Even today, the Spouting Horn remains a tourist attraction. People park along the rock wall next to the highway and wait to be sprayed by the salty sea.

Depoe Bay has long been a favorite destination for tourists. From the early 1930s on, visitors have come to Depoe Bay for sportfishing, whale watching, and to enjoy exciting coastal weather. This early photograph shows a small grocery store. Like many businesses, the store added gas pumps to the front of the building in response to the demand created by automobile travelers.

At this 1931 community fish fry, 1,050 pounds of fish were served along with coffee, beans, and buns. The gathering at the Bridge Lunch Café, built c. 1928, was sponsored by the Sunset Investment Company. In 1934, the café was moved back from the highway, and the Spouting Horn restaurant was built in its place. This fish fry was a precursor to Depoe Bay's annual Salmon Bake, which started in 1956.

COAST HIWAY BRIDGE AT DEPOE BAY, ORE   CHANDLER

For millions of years, the Pacific Ocean carved its way through the rock formations that form Depoe Bay. The result, seen here, is the world's smallest navigable harbor, landlocked except for the harbor entrance through the rocks. Conde B. McCullough built a bridge spanning the 50-foot gorge in 1926. Boats make their way to and from the sea through this narrow channel, known locally as "shooting the hole."

Commercial fishing has always been an important part of Depoe Bay's economy. In 1930, tuna catches topped two tons. Because of the dangers of ocean fishing, many fishermen lost their lives at sea. In 1946, the first annual Fleet of Flowers was held in Depoe Bay commemorating Roy Bower, Jack Chambers, and all the fishermen who lost their lives at sea. Here the fleet is at rest in the harbor.

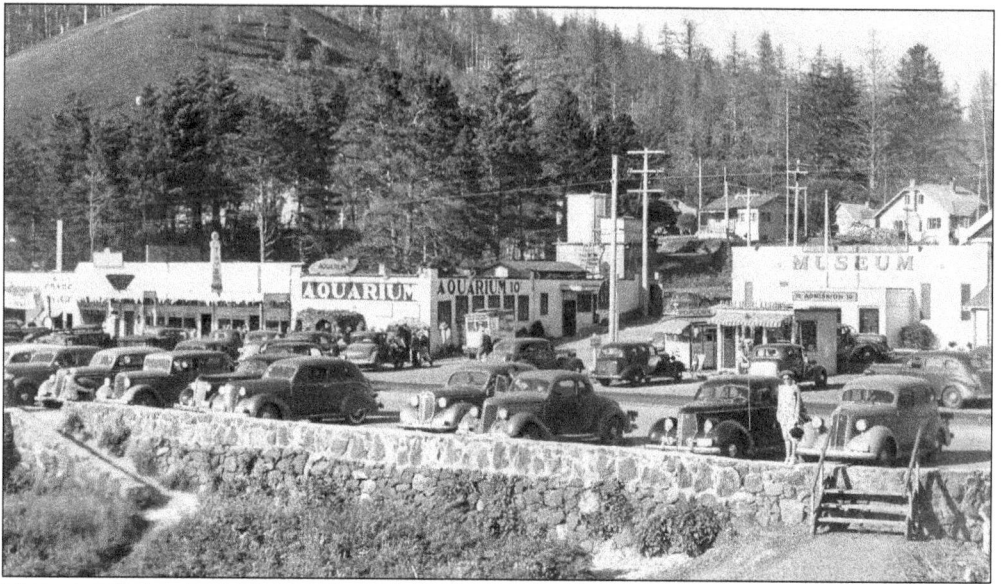

The seawall that lines Highway 101 in Depoe Bay, seen in this photograph, was built in 1940. The aquarium, built by the Sunset Investment Company in 1931, was the first in Oregon. It operated from 1931 to 1998, hitting its peak in 1939 with 120,000 visitors. The natural history museum, which housed the private collections of J. C. Braly and Ed S. Courier, included stuffed bears, deer, and birds.

The famous Spouting Horn restaurant was constructed in 1934 as a single-story building. In 1936, the business owners expanded the building to include a second story and added rooms to rent. During World War II, the building was used as a U.S. Coast Guard station and housed 40 men. Red siding was added in 1963 when a lumber barge sank and lumber washed ashore.

Four

TOURISM AND THE MIRACLE MILES

The first official Devils Lake Regatta took place from July 28–30, 1933. The event was sponsored by the Devils Lake Chamber of Commerce but was conceived, developed, and promoted by Edgar Lindley Merritt, one of the early movers and shakers in the Oceanlake area. Merritt's idea was to encourage tourists to visit the area by highlighting one of its natural attractions, Devils Lake. He thought the lake was the ideal venue for swimming and boating competitions, seen in this 1937 photograph. Boating teams and swimmers came from all over the state to compete. Jantzen Beach of Portland, the well-known recreation equipment manufacturer, sent contestants, as did other organizations that wanted to make a name in boat racing. Parking and seating for the first regatta was on the hillside property that borders the lake on Northeast Sixth Drive.

Attendance at the first Devils Lake Regatta was estimated at 15,000 people, with 5,000 cars. Crowds increased with every successive year until the start of World War II, when events of this kind were discontinued for the duration. Activities included motorboat races, logrolling competitions, and an illuminated boat parade. Foot races, picnics, parties, wienie roasts, band concerts, a golf tournament, carnivals, and dancing were also included to entertain spectators. Logrolling, seen at left, was done by both men and women. In later years, the event commenced with a parade through town. The parade centered on competitors and the Regatta Court and Admirals, but civic groups participated in the parade as well. The above parade photograph was shot on Highway 101 in downtown Oceanlake.

Boat races, seen in these photographs, were held on Devils Lake, one of the fastest lakes in the world. For decades, the lake held many of the world speedboat-racing records because of its location at sea level, a feature that makes boats move exceptionally fast. The first regatta was so successful that the following year a larger piece of property was found to accommodate spectators and their automobiles. Devils Lake Regatta Grounds on West Devils Lake Road was selected as the new site. During the 1934 regatta, hundreds of cars parked on the hill overlooking the lake. At that time, the property also had a view of the ocean. Today the area is Regatta Park. Although trees and houses block the ocean view, there is now a sandy beach for swimming and a playground built by the community.

Each regatta included the election of a queen and court of princesses who attended all regatta events and were crowned at a Royal Ball or Queen's Ball. Marion Klees, shown above with her court, was crowned the first Devils Lake Regatta Queen in 1933. The court was selected to represent individual towns according to who sold the most tickets to the queen's ball, while the court selected the queen. Regatta "Admirals" were honorary positions. Admirals acted as escorts to the royal court and gave a distinctively maritime look to the event. The crowning ceremonies were held at the Coaster Dance Hall in Oceanlake with the Salem Cherrians performing the crowning ceremony. A Regatta Ball concluded the regatta festivities. Twin queens, Ada and Ida Middlesworth, shown seated below with their court and admirals, reigned over the 1938 regatta.

The Red Devils of Portland, who did stunts on both surfboards and sea skims, enhanced the first Devils Lake Regatta. The Red Devils also performed swimming and diving stunts, and conducted lifesaving demonstrations. The next year, a local group of Red Devils took over, seen here clowning with members of the court. While these Red Devils did not perform water stunts, their outrageous behavior entertained spectators and contributed to the general sense of fun. The first costumes were made of red flannel, but the fabric had a tendency to discolor perspiring bodies. The president of the original Red Devils was called "the Big Squid." A regatta was held at Devils Lake each year from 1933 to 1940. The event was discontinued in 1941 due to war restrictions. In 1947, it was tried again but without success.

The Redhead Roundup, brainchild of Manville Robison, was a one-day local event first held in 1931. Entertainment was the focus of all the activities, which included comic skits and dances by coastal Native Americans under the direction of Chief Running Wolf. The idea was to attract visitors to the Taft area and to boost patronage at local businesses. Although it was only marginally successful that first year, the Taft Chamber of Commerce decided to continue it as an annual event. As the roundup became more widely publicized, it gained in popularity with each succeeding year. The roundup added activities until it became a two-day summer attraction, held annually from 1931 to 1941. By 1939, Taft hosted more than 25,000 visitors for the Redhead Roundup.

A large part of the roundup's early success lay in the novelty of "rounding up redheads." Contests of all kinds captured the imagination. There were prizes for the most beautiful redhead, for the plumpest redhead, the longest red hair, the most freckles, the shortest redhead, and so on. The most enthusiastic participants were ladies between the ages of 16 and 26, but there was no age limit, as can be seen in this lineup of redheads that includes a diminutive contestant. There was no stipulation that the participant live in Oregon, only that their hair be naturally red, and for that the judges took the word of the contestants.

At the first roundup in 1931, the focus was a redhead beauty contest, but there was also a grand sweepstakes prize for best comic stunt of the day. Prizes were given to three-legged race winners and 50-yard dash winners. Taft's Redhead Roundup took advantage of its location on Siletz Bay with a variety of water contests, canoe races, and swimming and diving competitions, with categories for both adults and children. The ever-popular Kiss Register, seen above, measured the intensity and passion of a kiss. Couples were given several chances to make the needle swing as far as it would go. Redheaded bathing beauties are seen in the photograph below with the town's brand new fire truck. Bob Ballard, fire chief, looks pleased to be behind the wheel.

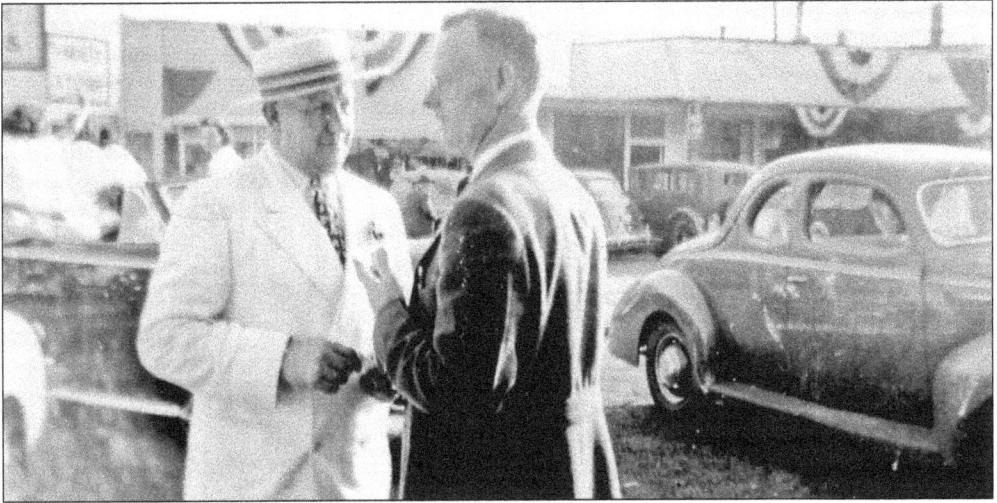

By the late 1930s, Sam Slocum, a Portland press agent, took the reins of the event and turned the Redhead Roundup into a real moneymaker for the town. Slocum, seen here in his signature straw hat talking with Manville Robison, was known as the P. T. Barnum of Oregon. Manville Robison conceived the idea, but it was Slocum who made sure the Redhead Roundup was publicized far and wide. Soon Taft's Redhead Roundup became a popular destination for tourists from around the northwest region. Summer traffic congestion on Highway 101 started as early as 1935, when the roundup attracted 15,000 people to the Taft area. The photograph below shows hundreds of people filling the street outside the Shop on Highway 101.

The Red Devils were a big part of the Redhead Roundup. The group promoted events and entertained visitors with shenanigans, including kidnapping redheads, holding mock weddings, and throwing people into the water in the bay. They dressed in red felt suits that, in the early days, often left the wearer's skin a nice shade of red.

When the roundup was in town, the whole town caught fire as redheads roamed the streets with hair that looked like the coastal sunset. It was all about fun for everyone, not just redheads. There was much to eat and a wonderful dance in the evening at the Oceanlake Dance Hall. This 1941 photograph shows the last Redhead Roundup winner, Selma McLeod, seated center, and her runners-up.

Mr. and Mrs. T. C. Gallagher and Loren Cleoworth opened the original Pixie Kitchen in 1948, seen in this watercolor print by Maude Wanker. The first restaurant, called Pixie Pot Pies, was located in Wecoma Beach at the spot where the Motel 6 is today. Primarily a take-home pie service, the Gallaghers started serving peach and berry cobblers on the premises in response to popular demand. Soon other items were added to the menu, and the restaurant became known for its "heavenly food." The more pixies that appeared in and around the restaurant, the better people liked it. The idea of pixies grew until they were being used on postcards, menus, and other advertising media. Pixie Kitchen postcards, like this one of a pixie riding a whale (below), have become desirable collectibles.

On May 21, 1953, an enlarged and redecorated restaurant opened as the Pixie Kitchen under the new ownership of Jerry and Lu Parks. Dinners included entrée choices of seafood, steak, prime rib, pork chops, or chicken. However, fun—not food—was the restaurant's main attraction. Features like the Pixie Garden (above) captured the imagination of young and old alike. The garden had all kinds of pixies at play, including large, wooden pixies mechanized to move, such as the mermaid pixie that flipped her tail. Often kids would hurry through dinner so they could run out and explore the garden while their parents ate and watched from their tables inside the restaurant, seen in the photograph below. The captivating scene of a pixie wonderland inspired the Parks family to expand the concept and open the Pixieland amusement park in 1969.

The Famous PIXIE KITCHEN – One of Oregon's Better Seafood Restaurants
Wecoma Beach at Oceanlake, Oregon – On U.S. 101

In the photograph above, the Pixie Kitchen is dressed in holiday bunting with the ocean in the background. While the look of the restaurant changed over the years, the appeal of pixies never waned. The Parks family continually found new ways to intrigue and entertain their customers. Extra attention was paid to children as customers, with "specially trained" waitresses, children's portions, place mats that folded into pixie hats, and surprise grab bags filled with candy and prizes. "Intelligence tests" provided at each table kept adults entertained. A novelty mirror placed near the entrance made a person look tall and thin, and read, "You Look Hungry." Another, near the exit, made a person look short and fat, and read, "Guess You Had Enuff." The artwork in this advertisement (at right) captures some of the charm of the restaurant.

119

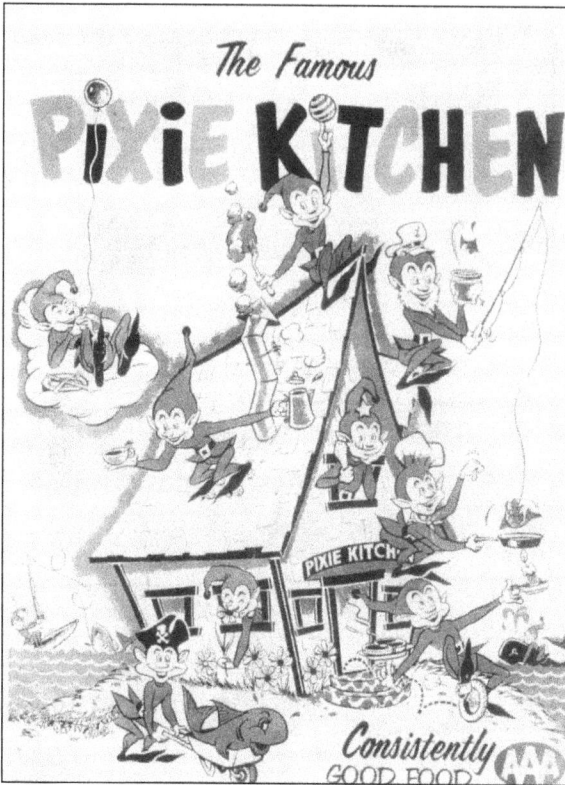

The Famous
PIXIE KITCHEN

PIXIE KITCH

Consistently
GOOD FOOD AAA

During the 1950s and 1960s, children did not have the myriad of amusements they have today. Those few businesses that catered to children and the whimsy in all of its customers were not to be missed. As soon as kids heard the words, "Come on kids, we're going to the beach!," they begged their parents to take them to the Pixie Kitchen. This delightful menu cover shows pixies at work and play.

As Oceanlake developed over the years, the Pixie Kitchen lost its ocean view and open grounds but not its charm. This 1970s photograph shows the addition of a cocktail bar. Called the Shell Room, the bar was separate from the dining room, and while it did not add much appeal to pixie lovers, it did bring in more customers.

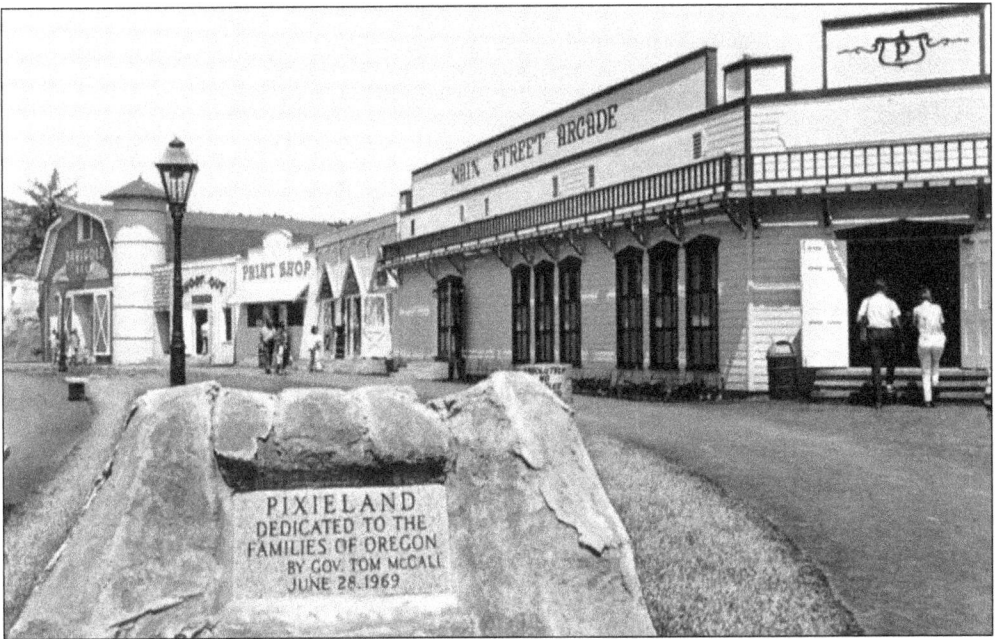

Pixieland, an 1890s–style amusement park, began operation in March 1969, just west of the Otis Junction on Highway 18. Situated on 57 acres of wooded land, it included fresh and saltwater canals, ideal for canoe and boat rides, along with additional rides and attractions. Pixieland seemed destined to become a major tourist attraction on the Oregon coast. Seen here is Main Street, which had a frontier theme.

This plat map shows the immense amusement park covering many acres. The rectangles on the right of the map are for campers. Pixieland promoters thought families would come to the park and stay for a few days while they enjoyed rides and shows, as well as fishing and other local attractions. Unfortunately, most people preferred to stay at the beach and visit Pixieland for the day.

Pixieland's Opera House brought in visitors and locals all year long. The Opera House seated 200 and advertised "five free shows daily" during the summer, with a different show every day. Performances included singing, dancing, and old melodramas complete with a mustachioed villain, a hero, and a maiden in distress. Some of today's residents got their first teenage jobs working as dancers and actors at the Opera House.

One of the highlights of the park was a log flume ride. The ride was adjacent to a Native American village and overseen by a 60-foot figure of Paul Bunyan. Log flume rides were later duplicated all over the country, but this was one of the first. Jane and Tony Harmon are seen here enjoying a wet and wonderful ride during the park's heyday in the late 1960s.

The Pixieland train, dubbed "Little Pixie," was a replica of an 1890 coal-burning steam locomotive. Train tracks wound around Pixieland for more than a mile. The 10-minute trip gave visitors a view of the surrounding countryside, showed them the extent of the rides and attractions available at the park, and took them past canals and boats on the Salmon River.

This 1969 photograph of Jane Mildred Harmon shows the unique roofline of many Pixieland buildings. Although Pixieland, known as the "Fairytale of Oregon," was loved by visitors, the park did not bring in the number of people necessary to keep it in operation. Bad weather and inconsistent attendance meant a steady loss of revenue. In 1975, the Pixieland Corporation began a two-year phase out, finally closing in 1977.

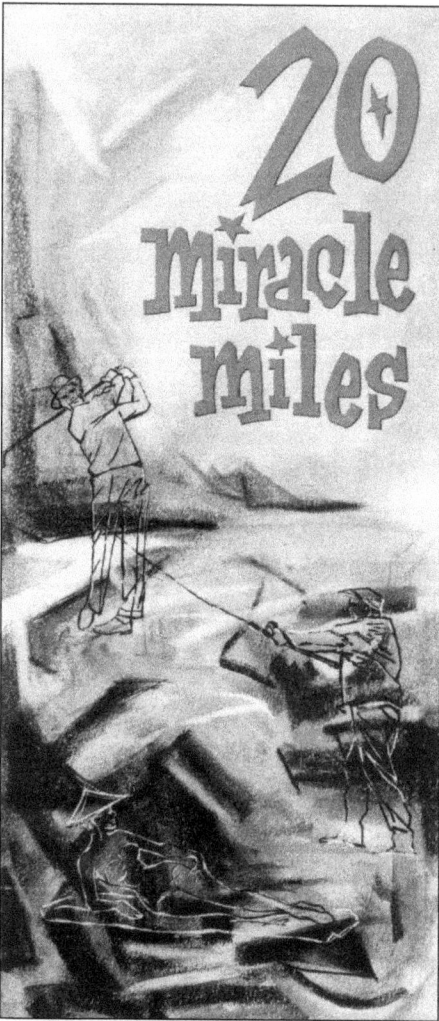

Along the north Lincoln County coast are miles of vacation, resort, and recreation sites once known as the "Twenty Miracle Miles." The area got its name in the 1950s when businesses began a promotional campaign to advertise this stretch of coastline as *the* destination for vacationers (above, left). In April 1956, forty-eight thousand visitors came to the area for a "Miracle Weekend." Along with the usual surf, sand, and fishing and crabbing activities, the weekend included a treasure hunt with real money buried on the beach, a kids' fishing derby, and water-skiing exhibitions. Later promotions focused more on selling lots for vacation homes. A building lot in Nelscott with an ocean view sold for $200. By 1959, lots for vacation homes on Devils Lake were still being advertised for only $500 each, as seen in this newspaper advertisement (above, right).

IT'S LINCOLN CITY NOW !!!

December 10, 1964

It's LINCOLN CITY by a margin of three votes ! The Taft counting board went over returns in that city a second time following Tuesday's election before a member admitted "Well, you beat us."

The returns, complete by 10 p.m. are unofficial and a recount may still be sought by opponents in Taft.

While results also were close in Cutler City, the vote there will be combined with Nelscott for official tabulation making the unincorporated area vote 158 yes to

Election returns by precinct were:

	YES	NO
Oceanlake #1	197	45
Oceanlake #2	146	71
Delake	198	98
Nelscott	85	57
Taft	115	112
Cutler City	73	69

Legal steps still to be taken before the new city functions include election of a council of seven, one from each of the five areas, one at large and a mayor at large.

will, as an early order of business name citizens to assist in forming a budget which must then be approved by vote of the people to form a tax base. Financially, LINCOLN CITY probably will not exist until July 1, 1965, start of the new fiscal year for cities. Payments from state funds certainly will not be made until that time.

State officials, in fact, may call for a census of at least Nelscott and Cutler City before releasing gasoline tax and liquor tax refunds amounting to nearly $10 per

In the early years of development, a healthy rivalry existed between the towns that comprised north Lincoln County. Each town wanted to be the biggest and the best in the area. Consequently, in the 1950s, when the towns began to discuss the possibility of joining together as one city, some residents were skeptical. Despite this initial reaction, the advantages of incorporating as one city became increasingly evident. All of the towns required the same government services, such as fire and police protection, sewers, water, and local ordinances. Finally, in December 1964, after several failed attempts, Delake, Oceanlake, Nelscott, Taft, and Cutler City voted to consolidate as one city, seen in this newspaper article (above). The aerial photograph below from the 1950s shows Lincoln City spread out over a long stretch of beach.

"Lincoln City"

Lincoln City held its first city council meeting on March 3, 1965. Shown above (from left to right) are council members Duane Griffith, Sam Cribbs, Carl Schmauder, Mayor Ross Evans, James Fitzwater, Carl Lierman, and Harvey Beeson. When it was clear that using one of the five town names for the new consolidated city would be too controversial, a contest was held to find a new name. Citizens did not want a "honky-tonk name" for the consolidated city, nor did they want a name that was uninteresting. "Lincoln City," submitted by schoolchildren, was chosen. The famous statue of Lincoln on the Prairie (at left) was donated to the city by sculptor Anna Hyatt Huntington. Gov. Mark Hatfield dedicated the statue, seen here at its present location on Northeast Twenty-second Street, in 1965.

Japanese fishing floats began washing up on Oregon beaches in the 1920s. The first person to discover one must have asked, "What is it, and how did it get here?" Glass floats were attached to fishing nets by the Japanese beginning around 1910. Over time, floats were torn loose to drift across the Pacific Ocean. They voyaged at the whims of wind and wave some 4,500 miles to a distant shore where winter tides cast them up by the hundreds. It takes a minimum of four years for a float to cross the Pacific. Most are round and have a slightly greenish tinge, but some are shaped like rolling pins, and rare floats are colored purple or red. Today Lincoln City has revived the interest in glass floats by hiding art glass floats along the beach for beachcombers to find.

Visit us at
arcadiapublishing.com

www.ingramcontent.com/pod-product-compliance
Lightning Source LLC
Chambersburg PA
CBHW050648110426
42813CB00007B/1947